THE END OF MARKETING
AS WE KNOW IT

THE END OF MARKETING
AS WE KNOW IT

SERGIO ZYMAN

HarperCollinsBusiness
An Imprint of HarperCollins*Publishers*

HarperCollins*Publishers*
77–85 Fulham Palace Road,
Hammersmith, London W6 8JB

www.fireandwater.com

Published by HarperCollins*Publishers* 1999
9 8 7 6 5 4 3 2 1

First published in the USA by HarperBusiness,
a division of HarperCollins Publishers 1999

A catalogue record for this book
is available from the British Library

ISBN 0 00 257128 5

Set in Garamond

Printed and bound in Great Britain by
Clays Ltd, St Ives plc

To Becky, Jennifer, and Jessica for hanging in there

CONTENTS

ACKNOWLEDGMENTS

It's impossible to adequately acknowledge and thank all of the people who have made this book possible. It is based on a lifetime of opportunities, challenges, and experiences. Without the people who allowed me to learn and grow and who helped me along the way, I would never have enjoyed such an exciting and successful career. However, there are a few special people I would like to single out for recognition:

My mom, who always believed that everything was going to be okay and that traveling around the world at an early age was going to be a good thing someday for my career. I didn't agree with her at the time.

Gene Kummel, who saw something in me besides those awful ties I used to wear in Mexico and gave me a break at McCann.

Don Keough, who from a lunch in New York at the Bull and Bear took me all over the world and gave me the opportunity to participate in some of the most exciting activities of The Coca-Cola Company.

Brian Dyson, who was a competitor first but always a friend, and who taught me a lot about what *not* to do, as well as what to do. Brian was always a special friend and adviser.

Roberto Goizueta. Only those of us who were close to him knew how great a man he truly was. I still miss him.

Doug Ivester. I'll never forget all of those Saturday mornings when I thought I was the teacher, and really I was the student.

Chuck Fruit, Dick Flaig, Mary Minnick, Chris Lowe, Dennis Kelly, Tom Long, Vinita Bali, Ian Rowden, Carolyn Jackson, Tom McGuire, and David Wheldon—the people who actually made everything happen and made me successful. Thank you, guys.

Katherine Schlabach, my assistant, for twenty years of taking care of me, and I mean it.

Nancy Cardwell, who worked with me on this book. I hired Nancy to help me with my writing, but perhaps what was even more valuable, she helped me with my thinking and Scott Miller, my best friend, my best inspiration, my best critic, and my best guide. Thank you, Coach!

Thanks to my editor, Laureen Rowland, whose vision has both inspired and challenged me throughout the creation of this book.

Finally, I want to express my gratitude to all of those other people who helped me throughout my career and, what was even more important, taught me everything I know. You know who you are, and I thank you.

PREFACE

Whenever I give a speech, I'm almost always introduced as the guy who was responsible for the biggest flop in the history of marketing after the Edsel—New Coke.

I love it. It's a great introduction because it sets me up for talking about marketing, and explaining why New Coke wasn't a failure at all. By the end of the speech, I've usually succeeded in bringing many people in the audience around to my way of thinking, and by the end of this book, I hope to have brought you around as well.

But, this is not going to be one of those whining "Now-let-me-tell-you-my-side-of-the-story" books about New Coke. Nor is it a book of propaganda for Coca-Cola or an effort to brag about all the wonderful campaigns I've worked on—Coke Is It! Always Coca-Cola. Just for the Taste of It (Diet Coke). Obey Your Thirst! (Sprite). That's because, as interesting as the history of marketing at The Coca-Cola Company may be, there's something a lot more important on my mind these days, which is that the era of marketing as we have known it is over, dead, kaput—and most marketers don't realize it.

There are still a lot of folks out there in the marketing world pretending that they are magicians. You know them, the guys who strut around the office looking smug and saying things like, "Yeah but, you're not in marketing, so you can't understand," or "Yeah, it costs a lot of money, but it's going to perform miracles," or "Yeah, I know you can't measure it, but trust me, it's working." Well, the days of the "Yeah, buts . . ." are over.

The truth is that marketing is not mysterious. It's not alchemy. It is a serious business discipline that can, and should be, carried out according to serious business principles. And if marketers don't realize that and if they don't change not only the perception but also the realities of what they do, then not only are they going to be out of work real soon, but the companies they work for are also going to be out of business.

I would have never written this book when I was still employed at The Coca-Cola Company. While I didn't exactly enjoy seeing my competitors keep missing the mark—because they were giving all marketers a bad name—there is no way that I would have said, "Hey guys, lemme open your eyes." So before the gods of voodoo marketing take the whole industry down the tubes, I want to raise the cry of alarm. Hello, out there! This is your wake-up call. I am not Chicken Little. I am the little boy who knows that the emperor has no clothes, and I can't keep quiet any longer.

I love marketing. I know that it can work when it's done right. And it's beautiful when it does. Simply put, the problem with marketing today is that for the past twenty or thirty years, marketers have become increasingly caught up with the trappings of marketing. They have been wowed by the glitz, the awards presentations, and the jetting off to "do a shoot" on some tropical isle, and they have forgotten that their job is to sell stuff. As a result, they haven't done a very good job of selling stuff, and they have tried to hide their failure to deliver results in a black box labeled "Marketing Is Magic." And further, because they have done a pretty good job of avoiding any responsibility for delivering results, they have lost their position at the table as serious businesspeople.

Today, at most companies, marketing is ineffective and therefore is considered to be strictly a nonessential activity. Many marketers and their bosses might not admit it, but just look at their actions. Whenever budgets are tight, marketing is one of the first things that gets cut.

My fundamental belief, and what I am aiming to show in this book, is that the discipline of marketing is a science and that spending on marketing is an investment that pays returns. As a science, marketing must be measured. It needs to be accounted for. And more important than anything else, it needs to be understood. If you think that marketing is just making eye-catching commercials and occasionally goosing up volume with rebates and promotions, you're fried. You will never succeed.

The good news is that the revolution has begun. As you are reading this book, you'll pick up the *Wall Street Journal* or the *New York Times* or the *Los Angeles Times,* and you'll see that one more company has seen the light and come to the realization that marketing spending has to generate incremental volume. The bad news is that the reason the papers are writing about them is that they have just fired their advertising agency or head marketer. And this trend is going to continue. Shareholders are becoming increasingly more serious about getting results and returns on their investments. So executives are getting a lot more serious about delivering them. And the marketers who don't get on board are going to drown in the surf.

My purpose in writing this book is to lay out on the table for everyone to see—both marketers and the executives who employ them—exactly what marketing is supposed to do and how it can be done. I will talk about the past and how marketing evolved into the sorry state it's in today, but I will mainly focus on the future and what needs to be done.

The way I see marketing in the future—the marketing that has already made me successful and is going to keep making me successful—is a back-to-basics marketing. It is grounded in the old principles of commerce. You spend money to make money. You only hire people when you need them. And when you hire people, they're supposed to produce incremental volume and profit.

I see marketing in the future as marketing that uses the same financial instruments that companies use to measure the success of any asset they acquire. It is also creative and adventurous. It may jar you and make you think sideways. I hope so. But it is not risky, because it also entails careful, scientific management of experiments. Some people have called me a "brilliant marketer"—along with some less flattering things. But, I'm not all that brilliant. I have just always had a destination and used logic to get there.

As I said, this book is not a Coca-Cola book, but it will include a number of Coca-Cola examples to explain and explore the strategies and tactics that allowed me and my team to increase the sales of an old company like Coke by fifty percent, to fifteen billion cases a year from ten billion cases, in just five years. I will show you not only what we did, but more importantly, I will also explain the principles that we applied in positioning, marketing, and revitalizing the brands. We did some exciting, glitzy ads and glamorous events and mind-boggling stunts. But we were successful because we never forgot that our goal was to get more people to buy more stuff more often, so the company could make more money. During that same period, the market value of The Coca-Cola Company jumped to $160 billion from $40 billion.

I will tell the story of New Coke and why it was a fabulous success. Yes, it infuriated the public, cost a ton of money, and lasted only seventy-seven days before we reintroduced Coca-Cola Classic. Still, New Coke was a success because it revitalized the brand and reattached the public to Coke. It didn't work exactly as we had planned, but it achieved our goal of changing the fundamental dialogue between the consumer and the brand. Changing the dialogue between the consumer and the brand is a concept that you will hear a lot about in this book. You will see examples of how this is done not only in the world of soft drinks but also in the worlds of computers, airlines, detergents, sneakers, and all kinds of other products.

I will talk about one of the accomplishments that I am most proud of, which is the repositioning of Sprite. Here we decided to fundamentally ignore the point that Sprite was a lemon-lime transparent drink and to move it into the much larger general beverage category. As a result, in four years its sales tripled. And we did it by changing only the extrinsics of how people thought about the product, without touching the intrinsics of what was inside the can or bottle.

And then there was Tab Clear. I'm not claiming that we put New Coke on the market because we wanted it to die, but we did put Tab Clear on the market for pretty much just that reason—Pepsi had introduced Crystal Pepsi. It was a new product in a new category that we didn't think was going anywhere. But it was going to take a while for it to die on its own, so we helped it along by introducing Tab Clear to reposition clear colas as diet drinks, which was a big problem for Crystal Pepsi because it contained sugar. Positioning is a two-way street. You have to position both your products and your competitor's.

I will also talk about Diet Coke, one of the most successful new products of all time. And I will talk about Fruitopia, which came about because Roberto Goizueta said, "Hey, let's just take over the noncarbonated market."

Further, I will discuss destination planning, branding, and why megabrands are a rotten idea. I will talk about the role of imaging and positioning, about assessing new products and new markets, and about research and getting inside the minds of customers. And I will talk about how to build a world-class marketing team and how to use it to accomplish all the things I've listed above.

Finally, I will talk about working with ad agencies. I think that ad agencies are essential to producing good commercials. But I also think that ad agencies are self-important, fixated on the wrong things, and overrated. I'll explain why and how I changed the relationship of Coca-Cola with its agencies. On Madison Avenue, I am called the Aya-Cola and Attila the Hun because I am a demanding client. But that's okay with me, because Attila was a results-oriented guy.

Overall, my message here is that what marketers have forgotten and need to remember real soon is that marketing is about selling stuff. Marketing is not about creating an image. Having an image just means that I know who you are, but it doesn't motivate me to do anything. Marketing is not about creating award-winning commercials either. It is about having programs and promotions and advertising and a million other things that are effective at convincing people that they should buy your product. For fast-food restaurants, it's about bites and slurps. For the airlines, it's about butts in seats. It is about profit. It is about results.

When I left The Coca-Cola Company as head of U.S. marketing in 1987, some people thought that I was fired, or eased out, because of New Coke. So they were surprised when I went back as chief marketing officer and senior vice president of the company in 1993. But I wasn't fired. I left in 1987 because I love marketing, and I wanted to do some things that the company wasn't prepared to do at that time. That's also the reason I left again in May 1998.

While I was away from Coca-Cola in the late 1980s and early 1990s, I had a wonderful time working as a consultant. It was like running your own test lab and going to school at the same time. My clients included convenience stores and fast-food restaurants, eyeglass shops, airlines, and even Microsoft and Club Med. From each one I learned valuable lessons about their markets and their customers, as I synthesized and adapted the things I had learned mostly at Coke, but also at Procter & Gamble where I started out, at McCann-Erickson, which introduced me to Coke when it hired me to work on the Coke account in Mexico, and at PepsiCo.

When Roberto Goizueta and Doug Ivester asked me to rejoin Coca-Cola in late 1992, I was hesitant at first. I was running my own business. I had grown my hair long and wasn't exactly excited about putting on a suit and becoming an employee again. But I had made a couple of mistakes. Because Doug didn't have a background in marketing when he became president of Coke, I had started spending time with him at night and on the weekends, talking about marketing, what it should be and how to do it. And as a consultant, I had also written a business plan about how Coke should structure and operate its marketing. In retrospect, it's obvious now that it was the longest job interview in history. Doug is a brilliant man. His energy and intelligence and excitement about making The Coca-Cola Company a first-class marketing company got me excited, and I'm glad he lured me back to the company.

I must confess that it was intoxicating to be called back to Coke, to do what I'd always wanted to do. And so I went. Off of parole, and back into the big house. Back to Coke. And the last five years at Coke were spectacular. Doug allowed me to hire the best people in the world: in fact, he encouraged me. I got involved in some of the most innovative and exciting ways of approaching markets all over the world. I traveled to over a hundred countries a year. And I learned the differences in politics and economics and consumer behavior from East to West and from North to South.

Some people found my intensity irritating. They mistook it for aggression. But what the heck? My theory was that when somebody comes in with a good idea, you should challenge him or her, because there's a real good chance they haven't challenged themselves enough, that they aren't yet at the height of their thinking. If you ask them questions and you push them, they will make the idea even better. I also bugged people by paying relentless attention to details. I learned some of this from a former consulting client, Bill Gates. At Microsoft, I named the process "push-back," any idea that was brought to Bill, he'd push back against it . . . and hard. But it was only to unlock the minds and maximize the ideas of the people who brought them to him.

I don't claim I came up with all the good ideas and that I did everything single-handedly. Roberto and Doug made the decision to bring marketing to the forefront and to make Coca-Cola a marketing company. It was all of us together, along with a fabulous staff. When I left The Coca-Cola Company on May 1, 1998, it had unequivocally the best marketing organization and thinking machine in the world.

All my life, I have been a pushy and inquisitive person, and much of my life I have spent working as a marketer. This book is based on all of what I've learned from all of the people over the years, from all the companies, from all the reading, from all the watching. It is a synthesis of the decades of learning that resulted in what I think are some pretty spectacular strategies, tactics, and processes. The stuff in this book is what enabled me to get to where I am today.

It's a place I like a lot.

PART 1

MARKETING IS NO MYSTERY

SMASHING THE BLACK BOX

The image pops up on the screen. It's Mean Joe Greene, the toughest, baddest football player in the NFL. He is injured, and he's blazing mad. In the midst of his roaring and raging, he spies a little kid holding a bottle of Coke.

Reluctantly, the kid offers him the drink, and Mean Joe takes it, politely saying, "Thanks."

Then, he gives the kid his shirt.

America loves it! People talk about it for weeks. The critics rave about it. The bottlers are elated. This ad is so hot that Coca-Cola marketers all over the world want to translate it. The Thais actually do a rendition with a famous Thai sports figure. The company should run it forever, right?

Wrong. Coke doesn't run this ad forever. In fact, Coke pulls the ad altogether and launches a new campaign called Coke Is It!

Wait a minute. Why would Coke do that? Why would it take a popular and award-winning commercial that cost millions to produce and pull it off the air?

The answer is simple. I know, because I am the person who did it. My job as a marketer for The Coca-Cola Company was to get people out of their houses and into restaurants and stores to buy more Coca-Cola products—and the ad just wasn't doing that.

A lot of people thought that it was a big waste of money to kill an expensive ad so quickly, but I did it because I had a strategic goal—which was to get more people to buy more Coke. What would have been a big waste of money is to have kept buying airtime for something that wasn't getting people to do that.

Marketing Is Supposed to Sell Stuff

This was in the early 1980s, the days when "image" was the be-all and end-all criterion of success for advertising and market-ing. I remember those days well. I also remember a new cam-paign for Sprite that was called "When You're Reaching for More, Reach for Sprite" that was also created around that time.

> **"I don't care about making award-winning commercials. The only thing . . . that any marketing person should care about is real consumption."**

It was introduced to the bottlers at this big extravaganza called "The Great Get-together" in San Francisco.

The bottlers loved the new jingle. So did management. So you can imagine their surprise when I showed up at the agency in New York a few weeks later and said, "Hey guys, the adver-tising is not working."

What gives? they asked. But again, the fact was: we weren't getting a sales lift from the advertising. Sounds like common sense to you, perhaps, but to them, I was the bad guy because—just imagine—I wanted to sell more Sprite.

You see, I have this screwed-up notion that advertising and marketing are supposed to sell stuff. So, it didn't matter to me that the Mean Joe Greene ad energized the bottlers and retailers, or that the new Sprite campaign was a hit at the "Great Get-together" bottler party. A marketer has always got to remember that there is only one target audience that matters—it's the consumers, stupid!

More than that, marketing has to move these consumers to action. Popularity isn't the objective. I don't want virtual con-sumption—the phenomenon that occurs when customers love

4

your product but don't feel a need to buy it. And I don't care about making award-winning commercials. The only thing I care about is real consumption. That's because convincing consumers to buy your products is the only reason a marketer is in business and the only reason that a company should spend any money at all on marketing. A campaign or promotion that doesn't get consumers to buy more of your product is, by definition, a dud. Buy my product. Period. If what you are doing now doesn't get consumers to do that, try something else.

The reason that I have named this book *The End of Marketing as We Know It* is that there are a lot of people in the marketing business who wouldn't have killed that heart-rending Mean Joe Greene ad. They wouldn't have killed it fifteen years ago, and they wouldn't kill it now. After all, they've been spoon-fed the idea that image is king. But the world is changing, and if marketers don't start changing now, they and their companies are going to become roadkill.

The Marketing Business Is Supposed to Make Money

Pick up the *New York Times* or the *Wall Street Journal* on any given day, go to the advertising section, and you will see article after article about an advertiser switching agencies or canceling a campaign because after x number of years the thing didn't seem to be working. After x number of years! Why wait so long? How about after three months! If it doesn't sell, pull it. Bite the bullet and pull it now!

"[Marketers] need to stop fooling around with the marketing-is-an-inscrutable-mystery hogwash and get down to business."

You should note that I don't just say "marketing," I say "the marketing business" because that's exactly what it is. Marketing is nothing but a business proposition. And to survive in the future, both marketers and the executives who employ them will have to start approaching it strictly as businesspeople. Forget the flair, forget the hype, it's a business and, as such, should be treated as one.

Twenty or thirty years ago, people used to say that they were in the "marketing game." Over the years, marketers have repositioned and elevated it to be the art of marketing. Well, it's not a game and it's not some decorative or magical art either. It's business, pure business. Marketing is about systematically and thoughtfully coming up with plans and taking actions that get more people to buy more of your product more often so the company makes more money.

I have succeeded in the marketing business not because I was just playing around, or because I had great artistic intuition. I have succeeded because I understand that it is business. I have approached every new campaign, every new promotion, and every product as an investment that has to pay a return. A profit producing business.

Sure, I have taken risks. You can't stay in business very long and you can't live without taking risks. Some of the things I've tried haven't worked out as I would have liked, but I have always performed a cost-benefit analysis of every marketing program. Big or small. I have rigorously tracked the results and measured the returns. And I have changed tactics when I saw that I wasn't getting the results I wanted because I have never forgotten that the purpose is to win new customers and to sell more product so we could make more money to reward shareholders for their investment. The most incredible thing that has repeatedly happened to me over the years was that I have endured from so-called operators and financial people an ongoing lack of credibility as a marketing person. You see, traditionally, marketing people were supposed to be net spenders. In their minds financial responsibility for a marketing person doesn't extend any further than staying within a given budget. My point of view is everything that a business does has to be aimed at adding value and making money. Marketing is no exception.

In today's world, with computers that can spit out data sliced and diced however you want it, it is pretty easy to keep track of what something costs and what results it is producing. Unfortunately, a lot of marketers haven't caught on to the implications of that yet. Many of them have figured out how to use computers in some very sophisticated ways to collect data, segment markets, or even to track some of the costs and occasionally some piecemeal results of a few of their programs. And then it's PowerPoint presentations all around!

In order to flourish, those of us in marketing need to develop a new way of thinking about what we do. We need to stop fooling around with the marketing-is-an-inscrutable-mystery hogwash and get down to business. The truth is that, if you want to, you can measure the return on just about every dollar you invest in marketing the same way you can measure the return on a bottling plant or a new truck.

There's Nothing Mysterious or Magical about Marketing

When I started out as a marketer thirty years ago, marketing was something that most companies did because their executives knew deep down in their gut that they had to do it. Maybe they weren't actually believers and they weren't really sure why they had to do it, but they were afraid not to do it. The marketers themselves told them that marketing was important. They

"It wasn't always in the best interest of marketers to explain what they were doing to their employers."

could see that when they advertised, sales went up. Magic! And all of their competitors had expensive marketing departments, so they thought that they should too. Keep up with the Joneses, you know. But exactly what those marketing guys did, how marketing worked, and even if a lot of it did work, was a mystery to most businesspeople.

Of course this was a situation that was great for the marketers. Their customers, that is their employers, didn't understand what the marketing people did, but they felt a great need to pay them lots of money to do it. So, since it wasn't always in the best interest of the marketers to explain what they were doing to their employers, they didn't. In fact, they did everything they could to perpetuate the myth that they were magicians, or better yet, practitioners of some sort of voodoo. When I first went to work for Procter & Gamble in Mexico, we actually had a lock on the door to the marketing department, and only members of the department had keys! We set ourselves up as this sort of creative elite that didn't have to deal with the poor stiffs working in operations. And since we guarded our information so carefully, nobody else knew enough about what we did to know if it was valuable. They just had to take our word for it. Trust us, we said, and they didn't have any other choice.

Now, I don't mean to suggest at all that marketers are, or have ever been, just a bunch of charlatans peddling snake oil. I actually believe just the opposite. I am a great believer in marketing because I know that it works. Not only do I know that marketing can get people who wouldn't otherwise choose your product to flock into stores and demand it, but I also know that it is not an optional activity. Any company that intends to grow and reward shareholders, any company that wants to stay in business, absolutely has to market. By the way, if you don't take the initiative and market your own brand or product, by default the competitor will position you (poorly I bet) by marketing theirs. But the point I am making is that marketers have wrapped themselves in this cloak of mystery for too long. The era of "Marketing as Magic," the era of "Marketing as We Know It" is over.

So, what I am going to do in this book is smash open the black box of marketing. I am going to blow away some of the smoke that wafts out, and let you take a close look at what is inside.

What you're going to see is not a collection of sleight-of-hand tricks or books full of mumbo-jumbo incantations. No rabbits and no hats. What you're going to find instead is an assortment of new and well-used tools. And not only am I going to let you look at them, I am also going to tell you how we used those tools to sell billions of cases of Coca Cola and other products. I am also going to tell you why we used them in the way that we did.

Because I've been in the marketing business and working hard at it for three decades—even though I only admit to being twenty-nine years old—you may pick up some new tips or strategies from this book. If you do, I'll be happy about that and glad to have made the contribution. But my goal isn't to write a script or book for *100 Winning Marketing Plans*. Rather it is to explain my approach to marketing and to encourage you to think about yours. I want to destroy the mystery around marketing so that everyone, both marketers and their bosses, will have to recognize what marketing is really all about, how it works, and how it has to work if your company is going to sell more stuff and make more money.

I want to open up a dialogue within the marketing community and within the business community (which I would argue are one in the same) about the whole concept of marketing. I think that a lot of companies are in big trouble today because everybody is just coasting along and acting on old assumptions about marketing. Those assumptions need to be reexamined. I want to challenge you to start that process.

I have thought about this subject a lot, and out of my years of experience I have developed the points of view that I am going to present in this book. I'm convinced that they are on target. So, as might be expected, I'm going to market the hell out of them to you. But the ultimate purpose is not to get you to buy into my thinking, but rather to light a few fires—maybe by throwing a few grenades—to get you to reexamine your own thinking about where you are today and how you are going to get to where you need to be tomorrow.

1

WHY HAVE MARKETING? TO MAKE MONEY

The sole purpose of marketing is to get more people to buy more of your product, more often, for more money. That's the only reason to spend a single nickel, pfennig, or peso. If your marketing is not delivering consumers to the cash register with their wallets in their hands to buy your product, don't do it.

A lot of marketers laugh when I say that. "Who are you kidding?" they ask. "Marketing isn't meant to sell. That's what sales is for."

Maybe in the old days, marketers could get away with simply bonding with their customers. You know the drill—shoot a commercial, add some soft music, and blow your budget on expensive airtime just to create an image in the consumer's mind. But today that isn't enough. Yes, you need to advertise and create images that you hope customers will like and remember in the store or at the register, but the only reason to spend money on them is if they help you sell more stuff.

A lot of people just don't get it. They are always going into rhapsodies about how a new distribution system, more efficient manufacturing, or an expanded sales force are really going to help the business grow or boost profits. But those aren't the things that produce growth and profits. You don't make any money until you sell the stuff, and you can't sell the stuff until you've gotten people to want it. And that's what marketing does.

Focus on Results, Not Activities

First of all, you have to understand what marketing is. Marketing is *not* advertising. Marketing isn't shooting commercials in Bali, or having a corner office with two potted palms

---

"When marketers understand that the goal is the selling and not just running promotions, they sell a lot more stuff."

---

and an ad agency bowing and scraping at your every whim. Those things may have passed for marketing yesterday. Many people still believe that that is marketing today. These folks may have fooled themselves and their bosses into thinking that spending a lot of money on creative advertising and running it on every television channel and in every newspaper and magazine in the world is marketing. But it's not.

Marketing is not even a combination of advertising and a whole bunch of other stuff added in, such as packaging, and promotions, and market research, and new-product development. Marketers do all those things. Those are marketing tools. But the tools are not marketing. Marketing is *using* the tools; marketing is deciding what to do and then using the right tools in the best way to get it done.

It's as if you have a hammer, a saw, a box of nails, and some lumber. You still need the carpenter to come in with the thinking and the skills to build you a table, and you need to decide if what you want to build is a table, or a chair. Marketing is a strategic activity and a discipline *focused on the endgame of getting more consumers to buy your product more often so that your company makes more money.* It is not just a collection of tasks that somebody has got to get done.

It is important to recognize this, because once you understand that the strategy is a key element in what you are supposed to be doing, it is going to change how you go about performing the tasks. When you think that your job is just about doing the tasks, then that is all you are going to do. If you are only task oriented, you'll think, "I've got to run five promotions, do six series of focus groups, and develop two ad campaigns this year" and you'll think you're doing your job—when you have really only done a few tasks.

The job of marketing is to sell lots of stuff and to make lots of money. It is to get more people to buy more of your products, more often, at higher prices. You're going to continue to hear that little mantra a lot in this book not because my editor was asleep at the wheel but because, as simple as it sounds, it seems hard for some people to get it into their heads. But that's what it's all about, what it has always been about, and what it will always be about. In fact, although some marketers will tell you it's impossible, the real job of a marketer is to sell everything that a company can profitably make, to be the ultimate stewards of return on investment and assets employed.

Sure, it's possible to sell more stuff if you think your job is just to run promotions. But, when you understand that the goal is selling and not just running the promotions, you end up selling a lot more stuff and making a lot more money because you do a lot more things, and are *smarter* about how you do them.

Understand That Marketing Is an Investment

When I first returned to The Coca-Cola Company in 1993 and developed the first round of television advertising, as a matter of protocol, I took it into Roberto Goizueta's office and played it for him.

"When you understand that marketing is what you do to sell stuff, then the money that you lay out is an investment instead of an expense."

"I don't like those ads," he said.

"Look, Roberto," I replied. "If you're willing to buy a hundred percent of the volume out there worldwide, then I'm happy to do advertising that you like. Otherwise, I've got to keep doing it for those damn consumers."

Of course, he got the point immediately. Moreover, from that point on, he told me, "Just show me the results, not the ads."

It's *all* about results. Just as Roberto wasn't the target audience of the ads I was showing him, seldom are you the target audience for yours. The marketer who insists that marketing is an art and says things like "you don't understand, I am the genius, I and only I (and my advertising agency, of course) understand my art. And, by the way, you can't measure it either" is done for. Marketing has to be tested and measured just like any other investment.

It's just as easy—and just as dangerous—to fall in love with your ads as it is to think they won't work because they don't "move" you. When I consulted for the Miller Brewing Company I found it incredible how everyone in the company had fallen in love with the advertising featuring the old jocks drinking Miller Lite. The ads had become part of the company's personality. Employees identified themselves with the ads. They somehow seemed to feel that their status in the community was enhanced by their affiliation with Bubba Smith, Joe Frazier, and John Madden.

There's nothing wrong with producing ads that people in your company like, in fact, it's nice if they do. It's good for company morale. But what the people at Miller forgot was that the people inside the company and the ad agency were not the target market. The beer drinkers and potential beer drinkers of America were the market. And because the people inside Miller were so infatuated with the campaign, they couldn't see that the ads weren't working.

They knew that they had a problem with sales, but they rationalized every which way they could to avoid changing the ads. They figured that since the employees, the management of the company, and the ad agency liked the ads, they must be right. And although it was true that a lot of the target audience of beer drinkers also said they liked the Miller ads, they were being motivated by something else to drink Coors Light and Bud Light. Remember the campaign: "Don't just ask for a light—ask for Bud Light"? Perhaps it wasn't as creative and charming as the Miller ads, but what mattered most was that it worked. It was straightforward and direct. It asked people to buy Bud, and they did.

Miller Lite was once the most popular and fastest growing beer in America. How is it doing now? What happened? The company didn't give people reasons to buy, so people didn't buy. What's perhaps most tragic for Miller is that this situation undoubtedly convinced some of the "nonmarketing" people at Miller that marketing doesn't really drive sales. It reinforced the notion that marketing is just a "nice to have," when you can afford it, but not a necessity—and surely not a "must-have" when profits are down.

The world is moving too quickly and investors are too demanding for companies to spend money on things that don't deliver a return. I don't know if there ever was a time when companies could afford to do that, but they certainly can't now. If you think about it, what most companies do now makes no sense. When they have a slow sales period, they cut back on the very thing that would increase sales: marketing. Why do that? Why do less of what is going to solve your problem, when you should be doing more of it?

At Coke, we had a policy that we would spend to sell. The only time that we would cut spending was if something didn't work and the brand didn't return on the marketing investment. And when something did work, we poured on more. We spent up to the point where there was no longer a return. When companies start looking at it this way and using marketing to drive sales, the slumps are going to be shallower, the peaks are going to be higher, and profits are going to be a lot more substantial. What does this mean to you? Well, when your boss begins to understand that marketing does, in fact, increase sales, he or she is going to stop viewing it as a nonessential frill and you can begin to use your marketing budget as a strategic tool to get where you want to go. Specifically, this means that your boss will learn to stop cutting marketing when business is slow and to start increasing it instead.

This brings me to my next topic: how companies set their marketing budgets. The traditional way that companies have viewed marketing is as an expense item. They set their marketing budgets based on how much money they want to spend. We've got x dollars, or we want to spent x percent of our revenue on marketing, and that's all that we can afford. Then they figure out how much advertising or research or whatever they can buy with those dollars. But when you understand that marketing is what you do to sell stuff, then the money that you lay out to do it is going to become an investment instead of an expense. The question becomes not "how many promotions can we buy?" but instead "how many more sales can we get?" And then "what do we have to do to do that?" When you ask it that way, you are going to decide that you want to make your marketing budget bigger rather than smaller, because you are going to be seeing proof positive that if you invest more, you can earn more.

Bear this in mind as you consider spending marketing dollars. Why? You should look at the alternatives. Evaluate what works. Find out what gives you the best return and spend there. Do that, even if it means spending on a show that's not your favorite, or even if you personally are not motivated by the promotion or the package. Spend there even if your spouse doesn't like it, or if he or she does like it. Your tastes and your friends' tastes don't matter. If something pays a good return, do it. If it doesn't, don't do it.

In the future, many executives are going to understand marketing a whole lot better than they ever have before (remember, they are reading this book too). Then, the only way marketers are going to be able to survive is to make sure that they sell more stuff to more people at profitable prices, and make sure that everyone knows it. Say what you intend to do, do it, and debrief to know the reason why it worked. And do it in the open for everyone to see and understand.

Create Demand through Marketing

Sure, you have to have manufacturing, distribution, and a sales force. But in the end, it really doesn't matter how well you distribute your product, how efficiently you manufacture it, or

---

"You can have the most modern fleet of airplanes properly outfitted with the latest seats, but you only make money if you put butts in those seats."

---

even how good your salespeople are at cutting deals if nobody *wants to buy* your product. A car company can be the most efficient manufacturer of automobiles, but it will only make money when the automobiles are sold. Think about it: where are the DeLorean cars these days?

You can have the most modern fleet of airplanes properly outfitted with the latest seats, but you only make money if you put butts in those seats. You can build a chain of restaurants throughout the world with the most efficient point-of-sale systems and the best-trained managers. But at the end of the day, you only make money if you sell more food for more money, whether it's hamburgers, tacos, or pizza.

It's the marketing that positions a product. It defines expectations and does so in a way that you can overdeliver on these expectations and delight customers so that they keep coming back for more. How many times a week do we read in the newspapers about yet another company that is closing two hundred stores or retrenching from x number of countries because they overexpanded? What happened? They went for the *Field of Dreams* approach—build it, and they (customers) will come.

But customers didn't come because the companies didn't market. They didn't explain why people should come to their stores, and they didn't ask for the sale. They didn't say why any one soft drink, motorcycle, service, or experience was different, better, or special. So they built it and nobody came . . . so they closed it. If they had marketed it, it would still be open.

Without this kind of results-oriented marketing, a company would get no new customers, and over a fairly short time, it would start to lose the ones it had. One of the maxims of old-style marketers is that if you get a customer young, you've got him or her for life. It's a comforting thought but not true. Preference is perishable, especially these days. Unless you come up with new ways of recreating or reestablishing that preference, of reselling people on your product, they will disappear—and so will you.

That's why the sports shoe companies constantly reinvent their products. They understand that young consumers today are bombarded daily with new information that screams "Buy mine instead of theirs!" Yes, you do need to get them young, but you have to keep on providing them with a new reason to buy your product. And another, and another.

Coke got that message loud and clear when it started losing consumers in the 1970s. It assumed that because Coca-Cola was loved, it was going to be consumed automatically. Guess what? It *was* loved, but it was not being consumed. The same thing has happened to many other companies that take their constituencies for granted. Converse shoes, for example, were once so hot. . . . Where are they now? What ever happened to Levi's? You couldn't go anywhere in the 1980s without hearing about and seeing Levi's. Sure, they're still around, but have you checked out their market share recently? Snapple, the miracle beverage of the early 1990s, came on like gangbusters and was supposedly going to replace carbonated soft drinks. What happened to it? People are still buying a lot of Coke and Pepsi, and even Fruitopia. But where's Snapple?

Nike is another example. It dominated everything in sports in the early to mid 1990s, then suddenly it's not as relevant as it was before. Almost simultaneously, this once-dead brand called Adidas comes alive. How? Adidas certainly screwed up by losing touch with its consumers, but unlike Converse at that same point, Adidas learned its lesson about needing to appeal constantly to its target users. It realized it needed not only to remind sneaker buyers that it existed but also why. In order to win the consumers' votes it needed to reestablish what had made it special or different (style, price, quality, experience) from other sneakers. And it did just that. Adidas has come back with a vengeance. With Phil Knight at the helm at Nike, I am certain that Nike will come back to once again redefine the sports industry. But the question remains, why did it lose relevance in the first place? It got complacent. Success is perishable; you can't take your business for granted no matter who you are.

Once you understand that there is a direct relationship between marketing and getting customers to buy your product, you will see that it is not optional. It is, in fact, a company's most essential activity. Everything else that your company does needs to be designed and implemented with marketing in mind. And if marketing is not at the very essence of your business, you're doomed. Your sales are not going to grow, and your profits are not going to grow. You are going to lose market share. And your competitor who does understand marketing, is going to blow you out of the water. They will de facto position you if you don't position yourself.

Sell Everything You Can Make

Ultimately, a marketer's goal is to maximize the company's return on assets, and that means selling everything a company can make until you have reached the point where the marginal spending to produce and sell the product won't yield the return you want.

In a later chapter, I will explore the implications of that and how a company needs to include marketers in all of its decision-making processes. That's because if you really want to maximize profits, you need to know how much you can sell before you decide how much to produce. For the moment, however, I will focus on current capacity and simply say that

"A good marketer will sell everything that a company has the ability to produce, the whole shebang, not just two-thirds, or eighty percent of the shebang."

the first destination that every marketer should be aiming for is to sell everything its company can produce.

Most companies build capacity to meet peak demand during certain times of the year, and then settle for letting that capacity sit idle during the rest of the year. Soft-drink makers are notorious for this, and most people in the industry generally accept that seasonal ups and downs are a necessary part of the business. But I don't buy this time-honored myth. Using production capacity that is already in place is one of the most cost-effective ways to produce a product; so, it's criminal to let it sit idle. A good marketer will sell everything that a company has the ability to produce, the whole shebang, not just two-thirds, or eighty percent of the shebang. The airlines call this yield management. In English, this means, sell every seat that you can, even if you have to discount.

The airline guys have it right. It's the only business that I know of where consumers pay less if they buy early. The airlines cover their fixed costs and they deal for full yield.

The conventional wisdom is that your share should remain stable from winter to summer, and from your high season to your low. People do high fives when they hold share in the off-season, and they do high tens if share goes up in the high season. However, the real opportunities for gaining market share and the easiest time to steal customers from your competitors is in the low season. Unless you already have a hundred percent share of the market, you should always increase market share in the traditionally low periods. That is because most companies make the mistake of following the conventional thinking. They figure that sales are going to be lower, so they cut back their marketing in the low season. But I say, "So what?"

Maybe overall demand for your product category does slow down in one season or another. But seasonal trends don't matter as much as you think they do unless you have a monopoly. Just because the public may be buying fewer airplane seats, golf clubs, or soft drinks in October, or February, or whenever doesn't mean that they have to buy fewer of yours. Make seasonality the other guy's problem. If you keep marketing while your competitors cut back, you can make, sure the products that customers don't buy are your competitors, and not yours.

Sometimes I think that the whole idea of seasonality is just an excuse that marketers have come up with and sold to everybody else as a way to explain away their own shortcomings. Research suggests that people's fluid consumption in fact does not drop during the winter. They may not be outdoors in the sun as much, but there are other reasons, besides wanting a break from the heat, why people drink sodas. Therefore, I think that it's up to the marketers to figure out what those reasons are and to sell their product to consumers. I must have gone to five Miller Brewing annual sales meetings and heard that sales were soft in the spring because of the rainy weather (p.s., it apparently wasn't raining on Budweiser those springs; it stole share from the guys crying about the weather). Some of the richest people in the world are those who simply refused to accept the time-honored myths of their business. Sam Walton would have opened a shop only on Main Street if he had simply believed the myth of local, high-touch/high-margin retailing.

I'm a great believer in self-fulfilling prophecies. If you think that you are going to fail, you will. People come up with notions, and those notions become institutionalized. I am sure you have a good deal of them in the company that you work for. So my advice to you is to demystify and kill them. But do it with the facts. (By the way, if you decide to test the principle of de-seasonalizing the business, remember that the marketing dollars that you have allocated to the current business are untouchable. If you want new volume, you are going to have to spend new dollars. You can't just spread the same number of dollars that you were going to spend in ten months over twelve months.)

If You Think You Can't Sell More, You Can't

I find it amusing how marketers always go immediately from talking about a great sales month or year to explaining why

"We decide that we are going to be able to sell x, and then we tell the manufacturer to manufacture that much. And we never sell any more."

they'll never be able to match it in the next month or year. You hear it all the time. People say, "We had a great year. We grew 17.3 percent," and then they spend a couple of months trying to explain why it is impossible to grow 17.3 percent again this year. The competitor was on strike, Easter came late, the local baseball team was in the World Series, and so on. Or maybe you just happened to have had a really good idea for a marketing program. What difference does any of that make? If people were willing to buy or use a product in those quantities this year, why wouldn't they be willing to buy and use that product in the same quantities next year, and even more, providing you tell them why they should?

The reality is that when you set low goals, they become self-fulfilling prophecies. We declare defeat when we believe our own story. We decide that we are going to be able to sell x, and then we tell the manufacturer to manufacture that much. And we never sell any more.

Think about if you were going to go into the retail pizza

business. You decide that you want to sell a hundred pizzas a day, so you call the people who sell the pizza fixings and ask them to send the ingredients for a hundred pizzas. They will calculate how much pepperoni, how much green pepper, and how many anchovies you need, and send that along with the dough, the tomato sauce, and the cheese. Then you call the oven people and rent an oven and the box people to get some boxes, and you're in business.

But when you open your pizza house the very first day, you sell only seventy pizzas. That means that you have thirty left. The question is, what do you do? You have two choices. If you want to sell everything you can make, you have to come up with a marketing program to sell a hundred pizzas and then some, in which case you will order another seventy for the following day. Alternatively, you can decide to make everything you can sell, in which case, since you have thirty left, you will order forty. The next day you will already have declared defeat, and you will sell no more than seventy pizzas.

Let's analyze both scenarios. In scenario 1, you would have to think real hard about things like what times of the day do you want to promote the purchase of pizza, whether you want other services like delivery, or if you want to sell some of the pizza in slices. You'd also have to analyze why people aren't buying your pizza and figure out what you need to tell them, or do for them, in order to get them to buy your pizza. This is destination planning. You have an objective, which is to initially sell a hundred pizzas a day, so all of your decisions are based on reaching that number. If you do this all of the time, eventually you will come up with a plan to sell two hundred pizzas per day, or three hundred, or four hundred.

Now, look at scenario 2, which is actually much more comfortable. You sold seventy pizzas on the first day, and if you continue to sell seventy pizzas every day, you may be okay (assuming that the numbers work to cover fixed costs). But you're only going to limp along, and most likely, you'll be out of business very soon.

Base your plans on how much you want or need to sell

rather than on how much you have been selling or think that you can sell. After that, marketing's job is to come up with the programs and ideas in order to reach the goal. This isn't "pipe dream" planning. This is about deciding what you need to sell to be successful and then finding a way to get there. Don't simply lower the goal to a more "reachable" number, because when you reach it, you won't be where you want to be.

Realize That the Bottom Line Is the Bottom Line

You can actually move a whole lot of your product if you give it away. How many companies all over the world have actually

"You absolutely cannot spend more money every year just to keep your old volume."

reduced their prices to the point where they are not making money? They are rolling in cash. Their top line is through the roof, but the bottom line is in the cellar. Volume is only relevant if it is profitable or actually creates sustained growth that is going to be profitable. In a later chapter, I will talk about creating value in the minds of consumers so that they will pay higher and higher prices for your product. But right now, I want to talk about how to invest your marketing budget profitably.

In marketing, you always have to keep your eye on marginal contribution. This means that you will have to determine how much you need to spend in order to sell incremental volume, be it pizzas, milk, soft drinks, seats on airplanes, cars, or dolls. You absolutely cannot spend more money every year just to keep your old volume. The cost of the volume that you already have should go down the longer that you have it. That's because once you have already convinced someone to buy your product, you won't have to spend again all the money you spent to get their attention in the first place. In order to grow, you need to shrink the amount you are spending on consumers once you have them, so that you can spend your marketing dollars on getting incremental volume.

If you watch television, you may have seen the programs on the weekends where fishermen teach you how to fish. On the show, when they catch a fish, they release it. In marketing, the objective is to catch the fish and to keep the fish alive, not to release it. If you want to grow, you have to move from catch-and-release marketing to catch-and-keep marketing. This isn't to say that you don't have to keep tossing out the line and pitching to your old consumers as if they were new consumers. You do have to do that, but you don't have to spend all the dollars that it takes to win them in the first place. You still need to give existing consumers a reason to buy, but you should be able to do this more efficiently.

Once you understand the difference between recurring volume and incremental volume, you then have to attach costs to each of them. This means that you will have to actually account for the spending that is done on the additional volume differently from the spending on the base volume. This is the only way that you will know whether the programs are actually paying out. The whole idea is to use your marketing dollars to have people who already use your brand to use it more often, or to get other people who don't to use your brand instead of whatever they are currently using.

If you don't build base volume, if you don't expand the reasons why people should buy your stuff, all you are doing is "renting volume." You need to own your volume. Remember, new users are expensive—they need a lot of convincing. Existing users are efficient, they just need confirmation of their behavior and new reasons every day to buy your brand. So break your volume up, figure out how much is base, how much the activity generated, how much is recurring, and then build your business plan and your marketing activities on that basis.

The people who are the absolute best at attaching costs are the people in the aerospace industry and the defense business.

They work on a cost-plus basis, which means that the way they make money is to add a percentage on top of whatever it costs to produce something. In other words, if they are going to make twenty percent on top of the cost, no cost can go unaccounted for. If they don't, then that cost will not be marked up, and consequently that cost will not be paid for. Every cent in a space or defense project must be accounted for. In marketing, you have to do the same thing. It's called activity-based costing.

Every single dollar in the marketing budget has to be attached to sales, and incremental dollars have to be directed toward activities that actually generate incremental and profitable volume growth.

Aim for Where You Want to Be, Not Where You Can Get

One of the biggest reasons that marketers often lack the discipline that they need to achieve their desired results is that they do not do a good job of defining what those results should be.

"Why pull a number out of the air and aim for a ten percent increase in sales when . . . a fifteen percent gain would put you in the (strategic) position you need to be in?"

This is getting back to my point that marketers focus too much on tasks and not enough on results. In the future, marketers are going to have to do a better job of what I call destination planning. And their bosses will have to demand that they provide a clear and objective result for the effort and money that gets allocated to them. Put another way: if you want to be successful, then you must clearly define, in detail, what success looks like. Then you've got to figure out how to get there.

If you go to the airport and you ask for a ticket, you know that the person behind the counter is going to ask you: where do you want to go? And you usually have not only an answer to give them about where you want to go but also a reason in your own mind about why you want to go there. That is because, unless you are just in a hurry to get out of town because the cops or some thug is chasing you, you would never go to the airport without knowing both of those things. So why do marketers go to work every day and launch hundred-million-dollar campaigns without having clearly figured out what results they are hoping to achieve? Sure they use big talk like "securing leadership of the category," or "dislodging the leader from its position," or some other lofty thing. But rarely is it to grow the bottom line by x dollars, or by selling x more volume this week.

Sometimes, companies are like the fugitive at the airport; they just know that they want to get away from where they are. They only want to solve their problems. They want to increase sales. They want to stop losing money. More often, they have objectives, goals, or even dreams, but they aren't well thought out, or they have been chosen for irrelevant reasons. I remember sitting through a business review plan where the manager put a plan in front of us and said this is my plan, but I also have an aspirational goal. His plan was well thought out, but it was his aspirational destination that was significant. But he had no plan to get there. No plan, just hope.

You may think that I'm just stretching the airport analogy here because I don't know if many people go to the airport and ask for tickets according to how much they cost. But I do know that lots of companies set their sales goals based on a percentage of last year's sales, or the size of a predetermined marketing budget, instead of figuring out where they want or need to be in the market. That's like telling the ticket agent that you want to go two hundred miles farther than your last trip, or you want any ticket that costs $122. Ridiculous!

The choice of a sales goal or an objective needs to be based on a strategic decision relative to market position, or on return on assets or some other overall goal of the company, and not on just as an increment over last year, or a decision to spend x dollars. Why pull a number out of the air and aim for a ten percent increase in sales when the strategy of the company says that a fifteen percent gain would put you in the position you need to be in to launch a new product, build a new plant, or subsidize entry into a new market? Make the goal fifteen percent, and then figure out what you need to do to get there. Or, why decide to spend $10 million to generate $13 million in profit, when you can earn $16 million if you spend $12 million? Decide where you want to go, and then build your objectives, strategies, and plans to get you there.

The important things to remember are that marketing is about spending money on activities that enhance the value of your product, brand, or service and give consumers more reasons to buy more of it, more often. It is an investment. It is not an expense that you have the option of cutting. If you want to grow, you have to market. And if you think strategically about where you want to be, you *can* get there.

2

WITHOUT STRATEGIES, YOU AREN'T GOING ANYWHERE

In 1982 The Coca-Cola Company rented Radio City Music Hall, hired the Rockettes, and with an enormous fanfare introduced to the world . . . TA DA, DIET COKE!!!

The product itself was a brave venture. It was the first time in history that the company had dared to put the vaunted name of Coke on a new product. But as interesting as the product was in marketing circles, the launch of Diet Coke was stunning for another reason. We were breaking all the rules about how to introduce a new product.

What had gotten into us?

According to marketing tradition, the way to introduce a new product is to start out in a small market, so if the product bombs no one will notice. But here we were, making a proclamation to the world, in the greatest city in the world. Why did we do it?

We had a strategy to position Diet Coke as a hot product.

In order for people—the media and consumers alike—to think "hot" we had to make it "hot." So everything associated with the product had to communicate hot-ness. Choosing Radio City Music Hall and inviting everyone in the world to watch was part of our strategy for communicating that message.

Take professional sports as another example. The New York Yankees, the Chicago Bulls, and the Denver Broncos aren't world champions because they are lucky. They aren't champions just because they've bought talented players either. Both of those things help, but they are champions because they approach their work in a serious, professional manner. Their coaches and players think about the game. They develop theories and strategies about how to win. They test them on the field or on the court, and then they refine them.

So should you.

Good teams spend a lot of time studying the competition and themselves, analyzing what they did right, and what they did wrong in the last game. Then they devise a game plan. The game plan is, of course, the detailed plan for the game: the tactics, the pass routes for football, or the pitching rotation in baseball. Professional teams don't improvise; they plan scientifically and execute. They debrief what worked and what didn't work.

If you want to win, you are going to have to do the same thing. You are going to have to have discipline, determination, and a well-thought-out playbook.

You are going to have to develop a strategy.

Know That Strategy Is Everything

Strategy is everything.

"If you want to establish a clear image in the minds of consumers, you first need a clear image in your own mind."

Think about it: if marketing is a business discipline, focused on selling the most goods and services at the best prices, it cannot be just a random collection of activities. Rather, it must be a systematic planning and development of processes that succeed in convincing people to buy what you want to sell. Which should not be misinterpreted to mean that as marketers we have to be right all the time. I've certainly tried my fair share of experiments (more publicly than most!) that didn't work—and we'll get into the need to revise your strategy, when necessary, in the next chapter. What's important is to build a strategy that is strictly focused on doing things that will increase profits by getting customers to buy more things at higher prices.

If you plan your strategies carefully and implement them aggressively, marketing will definitely get more customers to the cash register with your products in their hands. And if you want to establish a clear image in the minds of consumers, you first need a clear image in your own mind.

Take performers, for example. Some of the best marketers around today are performers and the people who manage them. You go to a rock concert, and they sell you a T-shirt, a hat, a program, a CD, all kinds of stuff that you really didn't need or want. They know that they have you captive for those three hours in that venue, you have a proven affinity for the artist, and you are ready and willing to buy (after all you shelled out fifty dollars for the ticket), so they use that opportunity to get you to give them more money. Those guys understand marketing. In the *Denver Post* recently, there was a great article about Bob Dylan. It wasn't about his music or his activities as a singer. Rather it was praising him for his marketing skills! Bob Dylan has figured out how to market his old albums to people of all ages, and he does it by pitching them not as golden oldies but as *good music*. And guess what, it's working.

Supermarkets, on the other hand, are a different story. Companies generally create products for the clerks to stack on a shelf. Maybe they go so far as to put up a point-of-sale piece, and then they hope. Yes, they HOPE that their stuff sells because they have manufactured it cheap, put it in the shiny box that the president of the company likes, and gotten it on the shelf. And what about marketing? What about analyzing the customers and communicating something that connects with them? They just aren't doing it.

Chart Your Course

A strategy lays out a target, sets some guidelines, and gives you a framework for thinking. A strategy allows you to use your cre-

---

"You can't and don't want to try everything. It would cost a ton of money, and . . . you'd end up getting nowhere."

---

ativity and to give other people the freedom to use theirs in ways that keep you moving toward your goal. In the end, premeditated strategies are what will keep you clean and focused.

To break through the clutter in today's marketplace and reach your target consumer, you are faced with an infinite number of possibilities, which presents a problem. You can't afford to overlook any of them, but at the same time, you can't and don't want to try everything. It would cost a ton of money, and besides, half of what you did would probably counteract the other half and you'd end up getting nowhere. So, to make sure that you don't miss any opportunities, you need wide-open thinking from as many people as possible, but you want them pulling together along the same road to reach a common objective. And the way you make this happen is by creating strategies.

Strategies provide the gravitational pull that keeps you from popping off in a million directions. To stay ahead of the competition, you have to be willing to take risks, to think up new concepts, and to try new techniques. But that's inherently risky, significantly more so if the strategy is not crystal clear. This means that everybody in the marketing department needs to clearly know what the strategy is. But it also means that everybody else in the company has to know the strategy as well.

This may not seem like a brilliant insight. "Of course," you're saying, "everybody knows that strategies are important.

That's why companies have strategic planning departments, executives hold big strategy meetings, and we all aspire to be known as strategic thinkers." If that's so, then why did a smart company like General Electric eliminate its strategic planning department? G.E. understands that strategy is so critical to effective operations that it can't be delegated to a bunch of staffers back at headquarters. But most companies do still have people designated as strategic planners. And this is a clear sign that they are just paying lip service and don't really understand that developing strategy, like marketing itself, is a core activity. Neither marketing nor the development of marketing strategies is an optional nice-to-do-if-you-have-time embellishment. They are crucial.

Don't Go to the Airport to Catch the Train

Strategy has to be at the heart of everything you do. I've already talked about destination planning and figuring out your objec-

---

"You can be blindsided by believing that volume is all that counts while you are actually destroying your brand product or service."

---

tive, or where you want to get. But once you have that, you then have to decide the route you are going to take to get there, and the so-called form of transportation.

Strategy is your road map. Strategy is how you plan to proceed in order to execute whatever it is that you decide you want to accomplish. The transportation vehicles are the tactics that you develop once you have chosen the strategy. For example, when Netscape introduced its Navigator search engine, Microsoft set the objective of neutralizing Navigator. (I have done some consulting for Microsoft, but I wasn't involved in the

Navigator campaign. So I am just talking about what I observed as an interested outsider.) The strategy Microsoft chose to achieve that objective was to knock Navigator out of the market by making it obsolete, and the tactic it used was to give away its own Internet Explorer.

The strategy has to come first, because the strategy is what determines the tactics that you need. If you have decided to go from New York to Washington by train, you wouldn't call a taxi to take you to the airport. And if you have decided to market your company's newest car as a sporty speed demon, you probably don't want to talk about fuel efficiency and a smooth ride for a family of six.

Having a strategy won't automatically make the tactics apparent. Once you have a strategy, you still have to spend endless hours testing and retesting, thinking about and refining your tactics. But what a strategy does do is to serve as a guide.

Everything that you do, every promotion, every piece of advertising, every single activity that affects customers—which is basically everything a company does—should come out of and drive the strategy ahead. And everybody who does anything that affects customers—which is basically everybody in the company—needs to clearly know what the strategy is, so that he or she can make decisions and take actions that will move you ever closer toward your goal/destination.

There are thousands of stories about how companies were able to make their businesses grow by increasing distribution, or launching a new package, or doing a line extension. The sad ones are the ones that have no staying power. The reason they didn't have any staying power was because their push was all muscle. They had no strategy. They didn't communicate the essential message of the brand, so they got a short-term boost but no real growth.

You can be blindsided by believing that volume is all that counts while you are actually destroying your brand, product, or service. The airline business has been notorious for crowding more passengers onto airplanes in order to fill the seats, which aggravates their core users and doesn't do a lot to build any kind of long-term loyalty in their casual users. One of the reasons why all of this happens and has been happening and will continue to happen is because people plan activities in the marketplace without regard for strategy.

Neutralize the Competition

Now that I have made the case that developing a strategy or strategies is crucial to the success of your marketing and your

"We decided to take the liberty of moving Crystal Pepsi into the diet segment, where it was bound to fail because it contained sugar."

company, I want to share some of my best-kept secret strategic weapons. Obviously no two companies are exactly the same, but specifics aside, the strategies still hold. One of my favorites was really useful in putting Crystal Pepsi out of business.

When PepsiCo introduced Crystal Pepsi, we at Coke set the same objective as Microsoft did with Netscape: neutralize this new competitor. We introduced Tab Clear into the same category we had launched Diet Coke in—but our strategies were completely opposite. In the case of Tab Clear, we went the traditional route, with sampling and testing in smaller markets. We gradually introduced the product around the country.

If this strategy was deliberate, what could we have possibly been thinking? Our job was to communicate that Tab Clear was just an ordinary product. It was *supposed* to feel like no big deal. Our goal was to kill the whole clear cola category by muddying it up. That way, consumers couldn't really get that attached to it, and Crystal Pepsi (and, yes, Tab Clear) would be products of the past.

Now, you may ask, why would we bother. Well, we didn't think that the category was ever going to be big enough to make economic sense, but it was an annoyance and a diversion of consumers' interest. Pepsi had introduced Crystal Pepsi to compete in the lemon-lime category with 7UP and Sprite. But as we at Coke analyzed the brand, it was remarkable how many of its attributes were diet-centric. Clearness, for example, is associated with lightness. The design of the package echoed that, and even the advertising had diet-category overtones.

From my perspective, Crystal Pepsi was just screaming for someone to reposition it.

So knowing how short-lived this category would be, we decided to take the liberty of moving Crystal Pepsi into the diet segment, where it was bound to fail because it contained sugar. By meeting a sugared drink with a nonsugared drink, we not only confused consumers about what the category stood for, but we also established an attribute standard that Crystal Pepsi didn't have. The strategy worked. Consumers never could figure out if they were supposed to buy clear colas because of what they tasted like—as a matter of fact, Tab Clear tasted nothing like Crystal Pepsi—or because of what they looked like, or because of their calorie content. So, very shortly, both Crystal Pepsi and Tab Clear disappeared from the market.

In reviewing my career after I had announced that I was leaving Coca-Cola in 1998, some critics said that Tab Clear had been a failure, or at least a disappointment. I can see how its short life span may have led them to think that. But based on our objective, it was a major success. In fact, I was quite proud of it because it seemed like a novel and elegant solution to an irritating problem. It's a strategy you can be sure that I will try again.

But for illustrative purposes, let's look at what might have happened if Coca-Cola had chosen a different strategy. For example, with the same objective of neutralizing the competitor, we could have chosen the strategy of going head-to-head with competition. In that case, the tactic might have been to introduce a product under the Coke name and use our advertising to do everything we could to clarify the category in consumers' minds in a way that made the clear Coke product more attractive than Crystal Pepsi.

If we had chosen to do that, I'm quite sure that we could have taken the lead in the market from Crystal Pepsi. The sheer power of the Coke trademark would have given us a great advantage. Witness what happened to Diet Coke. It was introduced fifteen or more years after Diet Pepsi but outsold it from the beginning. But, in this case, the potential size of the market just didn't make it worth the effort.

Kill the Category

A third possibility would have been just to ignore the newcomer, which is what Coke did for a long time with Snapple.

"If your strategy isn't working, as in the case of the strategy to ignore Snapple, you have to change it."

When Snapple came out, it positioned itself as the healthier alternative to sugared and artificially sweetened carbonated beverages. In this case, our objective also was to neutralize the competition, but this time the strategy we chose was to not dignify the category with a response. We didn't want to do anything that might suggest that fruit-based, noncarbonated drinks were even remotely in the same category as Coke products. Our tactic was to do no advertising that hinted at fruit drinks as a possibility. Later, when Snapple picked up steam and started taking volume from everybody, we changed that strategy and launched Fruitopia. The objective was still to neutralize the impact of the competitor on Coca-Cola, but the new strategy was to steal Snapple's profitability by entering the market with a noncarbonated fruit-based Coca-Cola product.

It's okay to change your strategy, just as it's okay to change your tactics, as long as you stay focused on your destination. If your strategy isn't working, as in the case of the strategy to ignore Snapple, you have to change it. But it's important to remember that when you change it, you need to make a decision to do just that. What I mean is that you should not just let your strategy de facto slip by the boards. When you meander into a strategy change, when you begin to just wander around and start throwing out tactics without tying them to your strategy, you end up with no strategy, and you are lost. If the strategy isn't working, you need to sit down and think and come up with a new one.

Keep Your Focus

Even if your strategy seems to be working, there will be many distractions along the way that will try to take you off course.

"Do something like this two or three times, and BAM! . . . you won't even have a plan to be disciplined about."

There will be opportunities that look too good to pass up. Or maybe you'll think you see a way to tweak something that you are doing to make a few more quick bucks, or to sell a few more cases or carloads of whatever it is that you are selling. But this is dangerous. If McDonald's wanted more people to buy Happy Meals, it made sense and was perfectly in line with that strategy to offer customers a cut-rate Beanie Baby when they bought a meal. But, after a while, somebody at McDonald's realized that they were making more money off of the Beanie Babies than off of the meals.

So what happened?

They started just selling the Beanie Babies.

It may have added a few dollars to the coffers, but it did nothing to win customers and sell more food. It was completely off strategy in terms of getting McDonald's to where it wanted to be (i.e., its destination). Do something like this two or three times, and BAM! your strategy is dead and you will never get to your destination. You will end up without any discipline in your marketing. You won't even have a plan to be disciplined about. You'll just be back to flailing around in the water and hoping that you don't drown.

Learn from Everything

Developing and following a strategy is what keeps you and everybody else on the same course so that you can maximize

---

"You shouldn't have more than one strategy about any issue, but you need strategies about lots of issues."

---

the effectiveness of your marketing. But more important than that is making strategic thinking a way of life.

"Strategic thinking" is one of those terms that people use a lot to indicate that they are important people who only think about big things and can't be bothered with the little stuff. But that's not what I mean when I say that you need to make strategic thinking a way of life. What I mean is that you have to think about everything. You have to look around you. You have to see what is really going on. You have to understand the connections among seemingly different things, and then you have to form an opinion that will serve as the basis for how you are going to act, and what you are going to do.

Any psychologist or student of human behavior will tell you

that this is how people naturally think and that they do it all the time. We couldn't live a single day if we didn't have opinions about the world and how things operate. We couldn't drive a car or cross a street if we didn't have firmly fixed understandings about how traffic moves. (That's why Americans have such a hard time driving or crossing the street in England. The rules we've fixed in our minds about traffic don't apply.) However, it isn't enough to do this subconsciously. You need to do it consciously, you need to do it all the time, and you need to do it in your marketing. You need to have strategies about everything, you need to know what they are, and you need to follow them. You need to always have a point of view on everything relative to your strategy and ultimately to your destination.

Once again, think about a politician. If a candidate is going to win an election, he or she has to have strategies about how to win the votes of various constituencies, including minorities, women, young people, the elderly, and voters from the other party. They also need strategies for dealing with the issues, like the economy, foreign affairs, education, taxes, race relations, abortion, and anything else that people care about. In marketing a product, you need to determine what the issues are for your product, and then you have to have a strategy to deal with each one of them.

Anytime you have an issue, you have to have a strategy. And, believe me, everything is an issue. You shouldn't have more than one strategy about any issue, but you need strategies about lots of issues. The more you have, the better off you are.

Understand That Everything Communicates

Strategy happens the same way that positioning happens. Meaning if you don't have one, your competitors will come up with one for you, most of which will likely put you in a defensive position and force you to focus on a whole series of random strategies (knowingly or not) that are unrelated to your business objectives. So I suggest that you develop one, as opposed to just hoping that one of your competitors develops a good one for you.

In all the years that I've been working, anytime somebody walks into my office, there are two questions I ask them.

"Strategy is the one thing that will keep you clean. When in doubt, just check whatever you want to do against strategy."

The first is: "What is the strategy?" And the second is: "Are we going to make any money?" I just don't think that you can go through business without being committed to strategies, and not just at the top levels. It's just as important—perhaps even more so—for your people to know and embrace the strategy than it is for you. Strategy is the one thing that will keep you clean. When in doubt, just check whatever you want to do against strategy.

Strategy has to inform everything you do. Everything that a company does—from the way it paints its trucks, to how long it takes to answer your telephones, to what the people in your factories tell their friends—communicates with the public. So everybody in the company needs to know and understand the strategy.

Strategies beget brands, and brands in today's marketplace transcend products. Brands are much more than what you eat and drink or brush your teeth with. Brand strategy is the summation of all your communications. Premeditated or accidental, you decide.

3

MARKETING IS SCIENCE

So now you know why you need marketing (to make money). And you know how to ensure that you do make money (develop a strategy). But what about the "art" of marketing? Ah, yes. Everyone knows that marketing requires an intuitive feel for customers, right? And that good marketers have an exceptional sense of style and drama. You know how many times I have heard comments like that? A million. And statements like those are just plain wrong.

Yes, there are artistic elements in some of the things that marketers do. You have to produce an interesting commercial that appeals to people if you want them to watch it and hear your message. But marketing itself is not an art, and it's not mysterious. It is about as mysterious as finance, which is why you need to start with a strategy. In reality, marketing is more science than art, and any marketer who wants to succeed in the future is going to have to approach it in a systematic and logical way.

Like a scientist, I collect data, I look at it, and then I change my activities to reflect what I've learned. This is a crucial point: you've got to constantly collect information, and you have to be willing to change your mind. If you know what your goal is, and you are willing to admit to yourself what the data is really saying, you have to change your mind sometimes, maybe even often. You don't want your airline pilot deciding before he takes off that he's going to fly over Omaha and then sticking to his plan when the thunderstorms roll in. And you'd think a political candidate was an idiot if he or she didn't hunt around for common ground with the voters. But for some reason, people think that marketers are supposed to pick a course and stick with it—

no matter what happens. That seems real dumb to me. Why not do what the guys who win Nobel Prizes do, try something new when you realize what you've been doing isn't working out?

If you agree that the ultimate goal of marketing is to maximize profit, to sell as much product as possible, to as many people as possible, as often as possible, and at the highest prices possible, then you must approach it this way. You have to be scientific. It doesn't make any sense to do it any other way. Why would you settle for doing something that delivers a ten percent return when something else is giving you twenty percent? And why would you do something that isn't working for even one minute longer after you found that out? Assuming of course that you try to find out why sales are up, or why sales are down, as opposed to celebrating wins with high fives and rationalizing the downswings with lame excuses about the weather, the economy, or maybe due to an irrational competitor's aggressive tactics. Debrief both success and failure and you win.

Get Really Close to Your Data

You may think you've been pretty successful so far without having relied too heavily on data. And I wouldn't be surprised if

> **"When you start really looking at exactly how much things cost and how much profit you are getting as a result of incurring those costs, you become a much better marketer."**

you were. Good marketing has always worked. If you position your product so that it is attractive to customers, you communicate well, and you give them reasons to buy it, they will. The difference is that in the future, marketing will have to be much more organized so that it can be measured in terms of both costs and results.

So what happens to the advertising awards that you get at Cannes every year? Well maybe we change them to the sales and profit awards and you still get to go to Cannes. So everybody is happy.

When you develop respect for the data, when you start getting more organized, when you start really looking at exactly how much things cost and how much profit you are getting as a result of incurring those costs, you become a much better marketer.

Measure the Results

By data I don't mean what you think. Every marketer you meet will tell you that he or she already takes measurements all the time. "We ran a promotion last year that gave people a pair of

"In finance, variance analysis is perfectly acceptable. . . . Why isn't this true in the marketing world?"

sunglasses when they bought a bathing suit, and we sold forty thousand bathing suits." We did blah, blah, blah and x happened. But that's usually about as far as it goes. When you dig deeper and ask them how did this activity help broaden the meaning of the product, or service, or how can you assure me that the consumer now thinks that your product is better than the one from your competitor, they usually don't have the answer. In other words, how is that investment you just made in that activity going to continue to yield positive returns through an enhanced relationship with consumers?

That's data. When you are focused on the bottom line, and are looking to figure out how to maximize sales and overall profit, you are going to know the answer. And you are going to use that answer to refine your programs and experiment to find the very best mix of activities.

In other areas of business, testing and revision is routine. In the finance discipline, when somebody puts together a project to buy an asset, both the financial people and the businesspeople come up with a number of assumptions, and they argue them at length. They run the numbers, arrive at some kind of financial model, and make a decision about whether a project should go forward. When we are building a plant, or buying a big machine, we go through the process of making assumptions and planning for maybe a year, or two, or three. Finally, the day comes when the building is built or the equipment is on-line and it starts producing whatever it's supposed to produce. We then watch it closely for a couple of months and measure the results.

If the results show that our assumptions were wrong, we decide that we need to do a variance analysis. What this means is that we actually analyze the assumptions that were made in order to get the project going and we correct those assumptions on the basis of new information, or results. Then we project on a going-forward basis what the new financials are going to be and make new plans based on that new reality. In finance, variance analysis is perfectly acceptable. In fact, we congratulate ourselves for having the foresight and the guts to change our minds and make new plans. And since the objective, rightly so, is to make the investment work, making it work is all that really matters.

Why isn't this true in the marketing world?

In the future, or better yet today, marketers are going to have to take the same scientific approach to doing their job. Marketers are going to have to make a number of assumptions, debate them until an agreement or at least an understanding is reached, and make a plan based on those assumptions. Then soon after the project, or brand, or whatever is launched, someone has to analyze the results and without hesitation, understand unequivocally whether the assumptions were right or wrong, and change them if necessary.

Change Your Mind

I know that some people will shake their heads in wonderment when they hear that Sergio Zyman, Mr. "I've-Changed-My-Mind-

---

"They [marketers] put their hands to their heads, listen for the voice of the oracles, and then unhesitatingly, take the absolutely most brilliant action possible. What a fairy tale!"

---

and-Now-We're-Going-to-Do-Something-Different," says that marketing is a logical and systematic science. During my career as a marketer, I have sometimes been accused of changing my mind too often and not being consistent. It's true that I played a big role in both the introduction of New Coke in 1985, and the decision to reintroduce Coca-Cola Classic seventy-seven days later. In the early 1990s, I sponsored the introduction of this great drink called OK Soda. It was going to change the face of soft drinks, or so said the research, and both the agencies and the management at Coke believed it. We spent a lot of money on it. We launched it with much fanfare, and seven months latter we discontinued it. Why?

Because it was not going to accomplish its objectives. We thought it would. We wanted it to, and we had a good plan at the time to make it happen. But it didn't happen, and we quickly realized this, based on new information from the test market.

We changed our minds.

If we had been more concerned about our egos than our shareholders we might have stuck to our original plan even after we learned that it was no longer viable.

It may have appeared to those watching that I was being

inconsistent. But the truth is, I always had a strategy. And I always had a destination in mind: to sell more products to more customers, more often at higher prices. Rather than be caught up in consistency, I have found it is far more important to be willing to try things that *might* work, and then test, measure, and revise. Change my mind, you bet! New info, new tactics. Same strategy. Fixed destination.

We once canceled Coke's advertising in Canada for a whole year and spent the money on new packaging. We did this because I came to the realization by looking at available data that Coke's generic packaging was actually doing harm to the brand. Advertising was not going to do the trick. I knew that the unique communication of the contour packaging was going to do a better job of distinguishing Coke from its competitors than having a bunch of commercials on the air. So we rolled out the new contour bottles, measured the results in sales, calculated the costs of packaging versus advertising, and saw that packaging was a better investment. But we didn't just kill the advertising, roll out the contour bottles, and leave it at that. We continued to watch sales very closely, and if the hypothesis had turned out to be wrong, you can be sure that I would have done something different.

Later in this chapter, I will tell you all about New Coke. A lot of people said it was a big fat mistake. It wasn't. I'll admit that it didn't play out as I had thought it would, not at all, but in the end, we achieved the destination that we set out for. Our overall objective was to revitalize the relationship of the brand Coca-Cola with consumers in the United States. We did research that said the public preferred the taste of New Coke, so we rolled it out. Then when the public said, "Well, yeah, we do like the taste, but we just remembered that's not the only reason we buy Coke. We buy Coke for the totality of the product, and that includes the fact that it's old and familiar and we feel comfortable with it." So we said fine, if you love Classic Coke, you can have it, as long as you remember to buy it. And they did. New Coke was incredibly successful in reattaching consumers to Coke and getting them to buy it. How it happened is almost irrelevant. Our destination stayed the same, but based on new information we quickly realized that our original plan wasn't going to get us there. And instead of winning more customers, as we did, we probably would have lost a few, maybe even tens of million of them.

Changing your mind is evidence that you are approaching your marketing scientifically. And that's not a cop-out. Experimenting, measuring, and revising are what scientists do to find the best solution. They try things and learn continually in the process. In creating the "I-Am-a-Magician" aura, marketers have over the years developed the expectation that the first thing they try in every situation will be—presto!—magically correct. They think they can put their hands to their heads, listen for the voice of the oracles, and then unhesitatingly, take the absolutely most brilliant action possible. What a fairy tale! And once you choose to pursue a course, heaven forbid you should change your mind, right?

Wrong. We all occasionally do things to shoot ourselves in the foot. But who in his or her right mind would stick to the course and continue to reload and fire into the same foot? When you refuse to change your mind, you miss the opportunity to capitalize on your learnings and do a better job of whatever you are trying to accomplish. You should hope that all of your competitors keep thinking that way.

The reality is that marketing, like science, isn't about knowing all the answers when you start out. It's about experimenting, measuring the results, analyzing them, and then making adjustments based on what you find out. I know from experience that marketing conducted scientifically produces better results. It gets more people to buy more products more often than marketing that is "intuitively" approached. The reason that Coca-Cola's volume rose from ten billion cases to fifteen billion cases from 1993 to 1998 is precisely because we applied scientific principles: assume, experiment, review, and revise. Old-style marketers can talk all they want about how alchemy can do the job and produce the gold. As for me, I am going to keep digging systematically for ore, assaying it carefully, and trying new veins to find those that are the richest.

But don't be deluded; being rigorously scientific about marketing is hard work and can make you very unpopular. When you abandon the old way of doing things, people feel threatened. Whether or not it works, people are comfortable with what's familiar. Some may even personalize this shift, thinking that you are rejecting *them* along with the old-style marketing. But keep in mind that the applied science of marketing is not about putting someone down, it's just about making sure that when you advance the ball, you have a plan, you press hard, and you keep going. You *must* be willing to change your mind in order to succeed.

The result is growth in volume and profit. I'll bet you'd take that any day! So will your shareholders.

Debrief Success

Equally important, and perhaps more valuable, than analyzing and correcting things that turn out to be wrong is analyzing and building on things that go right. Even though the people in

"But because they were ahead of plan, you figured that you did not have to analyze it ad nauseam. I want you to analyze success ad nauseam as well."

finance are very good about collecting data and analyzing problems, very few people anywhere in business are really diligent about analyzing success. We take success for granted. When we measure results and find that they are ahead of plan, we just decide that the assumptions we made were very smart and that we no longer need to worry about finding any additional justification for what we did.

When I worked for Coca-Cola, and as a consultant as well, I

enjoyed tremendously going to the field and asking the question, "Why did you miss plan?" only to find the manager, in some remote place around the world, try to explain to me that he or she didn't miss plan, that actually, he or she was fifteen percent ahead of plan. My argument was always the same: you're missing plan. The assumptions were that you were going to grow by x amount. You are in fact growing x plus fifteen percent? What happened? If he or she had missed plan by growing ten percent less than what you had originally projected, you would have analyzed ad nauseam. But because they were ahead of plan, you figured that you did not have to analyze it ad nauseam. I want you to analyze success ad nauseam as well.

One reason to debrief success is obviously to figure out what is working and why, so that you can replicate the success in other circumstances. But there is another reason to debrief success. Don't be blinded by your assumptions. Just because you run a promotion and it works doesn't mean that it worked for the reasons that you thought it would. For example, you run a promotion for supersize packages of detergent. You figure that it's going to appeal to women with large families who go through a ton of detergent every week. The promotion works. *Voilà*, sales climb ten percent, so you figure that you've got the large-family market nailed. But if you are smart and you debrief success, you do the analysis to see who bought the extra detergent; it may turn out that it wasn't the large households at all. Single males, who hate going to the grocery store and would like never to have to buy detergent again, bought the supersize packages. The huge packages appeal to their huge, he-man self-images. They don't mind carrying them, and their idea of meticulous decor means that it's okay if that huge package sits forever in the middle of the kitchen or the front hall. Meanwhile, you discover that the promotion drew very few of your intended customers in large households, which is in fact a much bigger market for detergent than single males.

So now you have two pieces of information that you can use. One is that you know how to reach a market that you hadn't thought about: single males. The other is that you still have to figure out how to appeal to large households. If you'd just said "whoopee" about boosting sales ten percent, you wouldn't have found this out. It is critical that you collect the data and you analyze it to make sure that you understand what is happening in the marketplace and why. Why is it that a commercial or a promotion that you thought was going to appeal to one segment of the population is actually appealing to a different segment of the population? Unless you debrief what happened in positive terms and in negative terms, you're not going to be able to learn from your successes, or from your failures.

You can't wait forever to do the analysis either. In order for it to be useful, you need to have the information in time to act on it. It really isn't all that helpful to find out next year that what we are doing this year was all wrong. We need to know it now, so we can fix the bad stuff and run with the good stuff. Marketing by month, and in some cases marketing by week, is really the way to go. At Coca-Cola, we eventually operated the business on a monthly basis. It wasn't easy, but when we did it that way, we found out what worked and what didn't, and consequently we poured on the good and stopped the bad in time to make a difference.

In the old, old days, marketing used to be done by the hour or by the day. If you talked to an entrepreneur who had set up shop on a corner on Main Street, he knew his primary goal: to sell merchandise. He knew exactly how many items he had in his store, how much money he had spent to buy them, how much profit he stood to make, and how many more items he would have to buy for the next day. In many ways, this new approach to marketing that I'm selling has much in common with this sensibility, seen best in the old, old days of marketing (not to be confused with the old days, the era of "image is everything").

I know, unless you are running one-day promotions, it's hard to run marketing on a daily basis. But consider a couple things: first, you should work to run your business on the shortest time frame possible. You may not get perfect information if you run it weekly, but you will get enough information for it to be worthwhile. And second, consider our friend, the entrepreneur. He knows exactly how many items he has in his store, and how many he needs to sell to make a profit. You can bet that image is the last thing on his mind. Indeed, the quality of his products and his relationships with his customers may be right up there, but what's the thing that keeps him up at night?

How to sell more and make more money.

Look Backward *and* Forward

Another thing that marketers have to get smarter about is conducting what I call presearch. Presearch is my term for hypothe-

---

> **"The old way of doing research was to explore the past to find out what was going to happen in the future. . . . nothing more than bean counting."**

---

sis-based research. It implies that you must explore *the future* (versus the past) to find out what's going to happen in the future. The old way of doing research was to explore the past to find out what was going to happen in the future. It was basically nothing more than bean counting. You'd look at what happened yesterday, at various demographic trends and trends in markets, and extrapolate what would happen tomorrow, assuming that history would repeat itself.

I haven't got a clue why.

I suppose, to a degree, this kind of thinking and research can be helpful. There is that whole "those who cannot remember the past are condemned to repeat it" sort of thing. But research stops short of coming up with the information that you really need, which is what consumers are actually going to do in the future. Certainly no one can "predict" the future accurately at all times—but presearch, or careful hypothesis testing, can help.

I used to think that focus groups were a total waste of time. At Coke, we'd spend millions of dollars only to have people tell us what we wanted to hear. In part, that was because qualitative research like focus groups is prone to bias. I remember when I consulted for Miller Brewing Company, we went to Sacramento and did focus groups on Miller Dry. We walked out with a set of assumptions, but we were concerned that we hadn't learned the truth. So we went to another research firm, gave them the same questionnaire, but told them that we worked for Budweiser. Guess what? The moderator directed the sessions to benefit "the guys from Bud." Just by saying that we worked for a different company, we changed the focus and got a whole different set of data. I'm not claiming the bias was deliberate, but whether it's deliberate or inadvertent, the fact is that the results were biased.

I still think that focus groups are overused. If you are going to spend $100 million on a marketing program, you ought to be willing to spend a couple of million on doing quantitative research that will give you more accurate data. But there is one valuable way to use focus groups—which, by the way, you can also use in quantitative surveys.

I discovered this method by looking at political campaigns.

I'm fascinated by politics because election campaigns are really short-cycle marketing campaigns with high stakes and fixed endings. You campaign intensely for six or nine months, then one day in early November, it's all over. The votes are counted, and your candidate either wins or loses. In this relatively short and finite cycle, quick collection of data and the effective use of information are essential. Every day, the candidate goes out on the stump, and the next morning the campaign manager gets up and says, how did we do yesterday? He or she collects polling data to find out if the numbers came up, or down, and looks at voter surveys to find out why. Both of those are research. A good campaign manager goes a step further by doing presearch. In other words, he or she asks voters: What if we told you this tomorrow? Would you vote for the candidate? And they keep asking until they find the positioning that is going to move votes. Then the next day, they do it all over again. Marketers need to do the same thing.

Own the Dialogue

The New Coke story is a good example of what research and presearch can and cannot do. Since I know that one reason

---

"Like a scientist designing an experiment, you have to ask the right questions."

---

some people are going to buy this book is to find out just what we at Coca-Cola were thinking when we changed the formula and introduced New Coke, I'll tell you here and get it over with.

I already mentioned earlier in this chapter that because the overall result of introducing New Coke was that we greatly increased the attachment of the American public to Coca-Cola and sold lots more as a result, I have no regrets about doing it. We set out to strengthen the bond between American consumers and Coca-Cola, and we did that, in spades.

But I will also admit that I learned some very important lessons from my experience with New Coke. One is that consumers are usually pretty honest in answering the questions that you ask them, but here's the clincher—they won't answer what you *don't ask*. Like a scientist designing an experiment, you have to ask the right questions.

The New Coke story starts back in the 1950s, when Pepsi seized control of the dialogue in the cola market. By that I mean that through its marketing efforts and Coke's inaction, Pepsi was able to define Coke's image. When Pepsi started selling its product in larger bottles, it implied that Coke was too expensive and that Pepsi was a better value. This tipped consumers off to the fact that perhaps price should be part of their decision-making process in choosing a cola. Next Pepsi started to differentiate itself from Coke in other ways, through its advertising campaigns. "You've got a lot to live and Pepsi's got a lot to give" told cola-buying consumers that Pepsi was about enjoying life. The "Pepsi Generation" became known for its youth, excitement, and vigor. Before long, Pepsi had defined itself by an image that appealed to the young and the young at heart.

Meanwhile, Coke wasn't doing much of anything to define itself other than develop a pretty flaccid "things go better with Coke" campaign. With Coke's help, Pepsi was positioning Coke as a less dynamic, boring drink for old people.

The next big thing that happened was the sugar crisis in 1975. Both Coke and Pepsi raised their prices, but when the crisis ended, Pepsi rolled its prices back in the form of occasional price promotions, and Coke didn't. Then Pepsi introduced the Pepsi Challenge, in which consumers in supposedly blind taste tests said that they preferred the taste of Pepsi to Coke. This, along with declining market share, is what really woke us up.

In 1979 to 1980, Coke came back fighting hard. We started challenging everything Pepsi said and did. We ran ads that used Bill Cosby selling Coke as "the real thing," which, of course, implied that Pepsi was inferior and underscored the fact that Pepsi was comparing itself to Coke because Coke was "the gold standard." We increased our feature activity in supermarkets. We redesigned our vending machines. Then we changed our slogan to an even punchier "Coke Is It!" We ran promotions and did sales rallies and a thousand other things. Heck, we did everything that we could think of, but Pepsi had done a pretty good job, and the dialogue was in their hands.

The big stumbling block that kept coming up in research was taste. At Coke, we ran taste tests too and found that Pepsi wasn't lying. In blind tests, consumers also told us that they preferred the taste of Pepsi to Coke, basically because Pepsi is much sweeter. At first try, people would get a smoother taste on a sip-by-sip basis.

Over the more than ninety years that Coke had been in business, it had never changed its formula, except to switch sweeteners and make other minor adjustments to reduce costs or reflect availability of ingredients. The goal had always been consistent: to make the modifications *without* changing the taste.

Ask the Right Questions

Now, because we ourselves had fallen for Pepsi's point—that taste was the only think that mattered—we decided that if we

---

"I think that maybe if we had changed ad agencies and started bombarding consumers with more and more reasons to buy Coke, . . . it might have worked."

---

wanted to sell more Coke we should think about reformulating it. We had thought that we'd tried everything else, and that consumers were not buying because of taste. In retrospect, I think that maybe if we had changed ad agencies and started bombarding consumers with more and more reasons to buy Coke, as we did later, it might have worked. But we didn't.

Instead we began asking consumers the kinds of open-ended question that market researchers often ask. Like: "Why is it that you're not drinking as much Coca-Cola as you were drinking before?" And they looked at us in amazement and replied, "But I am drinking as much as I *need*. I drink it when I'm thirsty, and I drink it when it's hot. I drink it when I'm eating a hamburger." And we in turn asked, "Well, what would it take for you to drink *more?*"

And they replied, "Nothing."

When we asked consumers what they thought of Coke, they would say nice things. "Coke is part of my life. It's the one that understands my feelings. It's the one that's been around for a long time."

But we were still losing tremendous market share to Pepsi.

Since the research questions weren't giving us enough to go on, we shifted to presearch. Instead of asking for blue sky answers, we started offering consumers alternatives. We gave them samples of various reformulations of Coca-Cola and tested them against the old Coke and also against Pepsi. We also asked them: "What would you do if we gave you a product that tasted better than Pepsi, but still was a Coke?"

They told us, "I would buy it."

"Would you like it?" we asked.

"Sure I would like it," they said. The problem was that even though we were asking them the right type of presearch questions, we didn't ask The Question. In truth, the only question we really needed to ask was: "If we took away Coca-Cola and gave you New Coke, would you accept it?"

Decide and Revise

Fortunately, New Coke did not turn out to be a total disaster. In fact, it turned out to be a roaring success for Coca-Cola, because

"Under the old rules, we would have built up so much momentum . . . that we would not have been able to admit . . . that we had a real problem on our hands."

it rekindled the relationship between the American public and Classic Coke. But the only reason that it wasn't a disaster is that we were willing to learn from the experience and to change our minds.

You are probably thinking that, given the overwhelming response to New Coke, it would have taken real numskulls to have missed the message. It would've been easy to stick to our guns and do more, more, more to try to rectify the situation, to prove that we were "right." But by thinking of ourselves as scientists and staying open to the data that presented itself, we chose to revise our strategy. If we had been operating under the old-style rules of marketing, we might not have had the guts to change our minds.

And we certainly wouldn't have changed them so quickly. Under the old rules, we would have been so committed to proving we were right, that we would not have been able to admit even the possibility that we had a real problem—or opportunity—on our hands.

It was because we had developed a scientific approach and mind-set that we were able to look at the data dispassionately and just get on with trying the next experiment, which was the relaunch of Classic Coke only seventy-seven days after the introduction of New Coke. Being able to stand up and say, "That was a mistake and I want to correct it" is more important and powerful than saying "I was right the first time and now I'm going to justify it."

Just think of all the great, free advertising that we got. Peter Jennings, the main anchor on the ABC television network, interrupted *General Hospital* (at the time, the number one daytime soap) to announce that there was a rumor that we were bringing it back. It led the news on all three networks, prompting Jennings to remark that "only in America can the return of a soft drink lead the news."

And yes, I left The Coca-Cola Company shortly after that, in 1987. A lot of people both inside and outside the company speculated that I had been fired, that I was the fall guy who took the "blame" for New Coke. While I admittedly played a large part in it, that's not why I left the company.

I left because by 1987, a lot of people in the company wanted to forget about New Coke and get back to doing things the way we always had. They were tired after all the uproar and they just wanted to settle down with what had always been "comfortable." But I was not one of those people. We had learned a lot from New Coke and we had gained a lot of momentum. We had been losing share doing what we had been doing before New Coke, and I definitely did not want to go back to that. So when I saw that I wasn't going to be able to keep trying new things and pushing ahead, that the environment just wasn't going to allow that, I decided I had to leave. I rejoined Coke in 1993 because Roberto Goizueta and Doug Ivester, who were then running the company, decided that they were ready to start moving ahead again.

Learn the Value of Listening

Although we missed the mark in our presearch before we launched New Coke, we did not miss it when we reintroduced

> **"We were acknowledging our consumers' power in the marketplace and openly bowing to their demand."**

Classic Coke. It was pretty clear that the public wanted us to bring back their old familiar Coke, but what wasn't as clear was how to get them to stop being mad at us and to buy more product. We needed to figure out how to position ourselves deliberately and how to communicate effectively. Again, we began in research mode by asking: "What is it that we should tell you in order for you to be happy?"

Not surprisingly, they didn't know. All we got back as answers was a collective whine of distress. So then we started testing some hypotheses and learned exactly what we needed to do. We asked, "What if I told you this, would this change your mind?" "What if we do this?" Nothing we proposed could save New Coke, because the press and the general public had made up their minds. But we had a real shot with Classic Coke.

Finally, we prepared a bunch of commercials and ran them

by some test consumers. The ones that we chose, because they were the ones that the consumers told us to choose, said: "We're not that smart and we're not that dumb, and we're bringing the old Coke back because that's what you want." They were wonderful because they gave consumers ownership. By bringing Classic Coke back, and positioning ourselves with this straightforward advertising, we were acknowledging our consumers' power in the marketplace and openly bowing to their demand.

Don't Forget to Ask WHY?

I talk a lot about science and about collecting and analyzing data because I think that marketers don't have enough respect

"When you understand why, it's a lot easier to figure out how to produce the what that you want."

for results. They have to start focusing on concrete, measurable facts and on delivering returns on their efforts. If they don't, they are doomed. But I don't want to give the impression that all you need to be a good marketer is the ability to track data, or in the case of presearch, to ask a series of logical "what if" or "either/or" questions. Tracking data and asking "what" questions are most valuable when you use them to frame the all-important question: Why?

Why? is important because it moves you from cognition to connection, from simply seeing what is happening to understanding the relationship of one event or trend to another. In other words, it's the difference between being aware of something and being able to take the information inherent in it and apply it to other situations. For example, after an election that puts a new party in power, you may see that people are much happier and more confident than they were before. This may manifest itself in their spending more freely, which is of course good for marketers. But you need to dig deeper and find out why, because it's going to make a big difference, not only in the strategies that you choose to use today but also tomorrow, when you will use the lessons that you learned. If the reason consumers are happier, more confident, and spending more freely is because the old government was lousy, then the strategies you want to try and the lessons that you learn are going to be related to getting out from under a lousy government. On the other hand, if people are happy because they actively like the new government and its policies, then the strategies and lessons are going to be related to the policies rather than the mere fact of change.

In marketing, as in science, understanding the why is the crucial step, because when you understand *why*, it's a lot easier to figure out *how* to produce the *what* that you want.

You Don't Have to Win Every Round to Win the Fight

You won't hit the bull's-eye and be one hundred percent right in everything you try. But even if you could attain perfection by

"Each round of the fight, or in marketing, should be seen as a distinct event that is linked to an overall destination. Make sure that you accelerate your ability to get to the end of the fight with more rounds won and less damage to your body."

investing enough time and thought on every effort, I'm not sure you would want to do that. If you only take the shots that you are sure will get you a hundred percent score, just think of all the points you will have missed by not taking the ones that would have gotten you eighty percent.

What we need to do as we go into the future is to accept the fact that circumstances change—that there is no such thing as perfect planning—and then get on with learning and improving as you go along. We need to get into the same mind-set that a political candidate or a finance executive or an airplane pilot gets into. This is to make the best possible set of assumptions on the basis of the information that we have, and then be willing to change those assumptions and change the actions in order to accomplish the ultimate goal. (Remember *Apollo 13*?)

To use another analogy, marketing is like a heavyweight fight. It is a long-term proposition. You can win a round, but it doesn't mean that you will win the fight. You may have a three-minute engagement with your opponent, followed by a one-minute period of rest during which you rethink your strategy, shake your head a bit, wash up, and go back at 'em. Even if things look good early on, and you win round after round until the fourteenth or fifteenth round, you can still get knocked out at the end. Each round of the fight, or in marketing, should be seen as a distinct event that is linked to an overall destination. Most likely you'll lose some of the rounds. Some you will tie, and others you will win. Use those one-minute breaks between the bells to rethink, to rest, and to reposition what you're trying to do. Make sure that you accelerate your ability to get to the end of the fight with more rounds won and less damage to your body.

Test and revise. Test and revise. You'll lose a few rounds, but you'll end up a winner.

PART 2

HOW TO SELL THE MOST STUFF AND MAKE THE MOST MONEY

4

POSITIONING IS A TWO-WAY STREET

You know that the sole purpose of marketing is to sell more stuff to more people more often and at higher prices. And you know that you have to do it scientifically. You have to have discipline, and you need to develop well-thought-out strategies to accomplish this. That's pretty good advice for anybody doing anything in business.

Now let's get down to the nitty-gritty specifics, to the stuff that's at the heart of marketing that I don't think most marketers think very clearly about. It's time to talk about building brands, positioning products, and creating images for those brands and products—and how you need to do these things differently in order to succeed in today's (and tomorrow's) supercompetitive marketplace.

How Branding Creates Identity

Even though you think you know what branding is, humor me by thinking back to the original use of the term. Yes, folks, we're talking cowboys and, not indians, but cattle.

> **"Johnny Carson was a brand whose elements included the monologue . . . the golf swing, his interchanges with Ed McMahon, and Carnac the Magnificent."**

The cowboys on the plains would heat up their branding irons and then use them to mark their cattle with their signature mark, whether it was an *X*, a circle, or what have you. Why? So there was no confusion over who owned what. Over time, these brands came to serve as identifiers not only for the owners, but also for buyers. Buyers came to understand (and remember) that when they bought the cattle marked with the circle and the *X*, they tended to be fat and well fed. The ones with the double bars, on the other hand, were stringy and tough.

Coca-Cola is the original, the real thing. Pepsi is the insurgent, the choice of change. McDonald's is Ronald. Burger King is broiling versus frying.

Another way of looking at branding is to think about yourself and your name. My brand is Sergio Zyman. It specifies me and is a shorthand way of evoking in your mind all of the qualities that you associate with me. Johnny Carson was a brand whose elements included the monologue at the beginning of every show, his mannerisms, the golf swing, his interchanges with Ed McMahon, and Carnac the Magnificent. When you saw his face or heard his name, up popped a whole set of assumptions and beliefs that you had developed about him over time. You expected to be entertained and amused in a slightly zany but sophisticated way.

The whole reason for creating a brand is to get consumers to identify a number of desirable qualities and traits with your specific product. Coca-Cola is refreshing, delicious, and good tasting. But that's not all. It also has a lot of other traits that are based on the relationship that the brand has built with people over time. It has its heritage and the mystique of being quintessentially American. We remember our childhood experiences and what our parents told us about Coke. There are the thoughts we have about other Coke drinkers, and memories connected with consuming Coke. Diet Coke is a diet version of Coke, but again it is much more than that. It's a reflection of how I feel or want to feel and how I look and want to look.

If you were a street vendor selling fruits and vegetables, you could take your pushcart out and go to a different corner every morning and start hawking your wares to a new audience every day. This would expose you to a lot more people than if you just stood at the corner of Main Street and Grand Avenue. But you would soon realize that this was a pretty inefficient way to operate, because every day you would have to attract the attention of people who had never seen you before and convince them to try your stuff. You wouldn't have built up any residual goodwill. You would be marketing horizontally, which means you would be entering new markets, rather than incrementally, by selling more to established customers. And your costs would be very high.

Incremental marketing is much cheaper than horizontal marketing. You can spend less and sell more. You still have to spend on refreshing your brands, reminding people why they like your stuff, and giving them more reasons to buy it. If you want people to buy your product every day, you have to market every day, and if you want them to buy more, you have to give them more reasons. But it is much more efficient to build relationships with consumers and then work on getting the people who know you to buy more stuff than it is to go out and find new consumers every day.

Why Megabrands Are a Rotten Idea

Marketing is full of terms that should be clear and obvious because they are words—like brands or trademarks—that marketing people use every day. But if you actually ask your colleagues to stop throwing them around loosely and define what they mean, you'll get a lot of fuzzy or conflicting replies.

"Megabranding takes away the uniqueness and says in effect, 'Look, all of our products are basically the same.'"

Some of the greatest confusion seems to be found around trademarks and brands because they often have the same name. For example, Coca-Cola is the name and the trademark of the world's largest soft-drink company, but it is also the name of its flagship brand, which is a different brand from Diet Coke, Cherry Coke, Sprite, or Fruitopia. This confusion of brands with trademarks is one of the reasons that so many companies bought into the concept of megabrands, which is a really stupid concept.

The whole purpose of branding is to *differentiate* your product in the marketplace and to get consumers to identify it as different, better, and special. That's why marketers spend tons of money explaining how Tide is different from Cheer, how Lipton is different from Nestlé, how Goodyear is different from Michelin. The aim is to develop a unique selling proposition.

Which is precisely why megabrands are such a bad idea.

The false premise behind megabrands is that you can actually market a series of different products as the same product. At one point we had a recommendation from a major design firm that we should market Coke, Diet Coke, Cherry Coke, Caffeine-Free Diet Coke, and all the rest of our beverages under one umbrella. A megabrand! What a great idea! Make obsolete each one of the unique and differentiated elements that we had worked so hard to create for each brand by simply lumping them all together and saying: by the way, all of these brands are basically the same. You should drink them whenever you feel like having a Coke product.

How meaningful to a consumer is that?

The way to get people to choose your product over anybody else's is by explaining to them how your product is different, better, and special. Sure, the Coca-Cola trademark has an image of quality that says: you'll pay a bit more for a Coca-Cola product, because you know more about our taste and quality than you do about the generic product. But a Diet Coke is not a regular Coke is not a Cherry Coke. Different people drink them, and they drink them for different reasons and at different times. What appeals to Diet Coke drinkers isn't what's going to appeal to Coke drinkers or to Cherry Coke drinkers. So it is plain ridiculous to think that you can market them all in the same way.

Megabranding takes away the uniqueness and says in effect, "Look, all of our products are basically the same, so just pick one of them."

Trademarks, which are essentially what megabrands are trying to sell, do have a value in softening up consumers and getting them to be willing to listen to the other things that you have to say. "I trust Coke, Kellogg's, Toyota, Compaq, or whoever, so I don't have to worry about quality. I can make my decision on other bases." But as a marketer, you have to define those other bases. You have to make each product distinctive in consumers' minds so they will recognize it as something they like and will buy over and over again.

In order to do this, you have to differentiate in relative terms to the competitive offering. In order to do this, you have to consider what other choices consumers have. The reasons that people buy Kellogg's Raisin Bran are not the same reasons that people buy Kellogg's Frosted Flakes. Each brand appeals to different people for different reasons, and consumers buy them at different times for different purposes. So you can't motivate everybody to buy all of your products with a one-size-fits-all approach. One size—or one brand, no matter how big and all-encompassing it tries to be—does not fit all people or all products.

Differentiation is critical; sameness has no value.

Because branding is about creating strong identities, at some point, you have to recognize that an identity you create is not going to appeal to some customers, or it is going to appeal, but will perhaps be out of their reach. Most people think Ferraris are pretty spectacular cars, but not many of them are going to find the money to buy one. At Coke, we always said that we needed to be different, better, and special. So even when consumers chose a different brand, we wanted to make sure that those consumers understood that Coca-Cola was indeed different, better, and special. When they made their choice, we wanted them to do it consciously, and to know when they were not choosing Coke.

Think about the last time you or someone you know ordered a Coke in a restaurant. You don't say, "I'd like a cola, please." You say, "I'll have a Coke." You're making a distinction. Perhaps even more significant, though, is when the server replies, "Sorry, we don't have Coke. Is Pepsi all right?" There's a distinction in the mind of the server as well, causing him to double-check that you'll accept something that isn't "the real thing."

The name, the expectation, the distinction. That's branding.

Why Brands Aren't Static

Branding is tricky because you want to sell as much of your product to as many people as possible, but at the same time

---

"The Club Med people fell asleep at the switch–they didn't evolve."

---

each brand has to be built on a unique selling proposition. You want to convince more and more people that your brand and its selling propositions are attractive and different, so you want to continually broaden its appeal but you don't want to lose its uniqueness.

The worst thing you can do is think that you can just introduce a brand and leave it there. If you do this, you are not going to sell a lot of product. One reason for this is that you are going to miss a lot of sales if you don't continually give people new ways to look at your brand. Look at Arm & Hammer Baking Soda. The product is what it is, but they changed the meaning of what the brand was. They changed the area of competition. They said, baking soda is not just for putting in biscuits, which is what everyone used to think. It's also for freshening the air in your refrigerator, cleaning your teeth, washing the bathtub, and making your heartburn go away. Heck, they even convinced us that you should pour it in the sink to keep the sink fresh! Is that brilliant or what? Buy it and pour it out! What a concept! Over and over, they have redefined the consumer offering, and it has made them very successful.

Another reason that you have to keep defining and redefining your brand is that as soon as you come up with something new, especially something that works, everybody else is going to copy it. You say your product will make my hair silkier because of some special ingredient. So everybody else adds the ingredient and says "Me too. Mine will do the same thing." I like to tell people that the status quo is like a ramp or a hill. You set your product on it and let go, and it rolls down. You've got to keep doing things to push it back up and reestablish its unique value.

Among my clients when I was a consultant was Club Med. The concept behind Club Med was fabulous. It was the antidote to civilization. The proposition was that people could go away and do the things that they dreamed about doing, like scuba diving, snorkeling, wind sailing, or samba dancing, in a structured environment that seemed unstructured. The idea was that it was not going to be luxurious but it was going to be fun. You didn't have to carry any money around (the food was free and the drinks were bought with "bar beads"), and you could bond with a great group of strangers without having to comply with any rules and regulations.

It was so successful for so long that it attracted a tremendous number of competitors who came in and said, "Hey, we can offer the same as Club Med, but for less." The Club Med people fell asleep at the switch—they didn't evolve. They grew because they kept opening villages. The management system in the villages was fantastic. It was about entertaining the people and giving them great food and making sure that the G.O.s, who were the people that took care of the guests, were properly hired and trained. Where the flaw was, in my opinion and as I have said many times, was in the fact that the company was run the same way—like a series of villages, not like a company. The very same thing that made the club successful, which was its informality and fun-loving spirit, was not good for profitability.

Club Med forgot that it needed to stay different because it was once peerless in its category. It allowed the competition to create sameness and, in some ways, to beat Club Med at its own game.

What is to be learned here? You need to constantly challenge your own concept, even if you are proud of what you have created, even if it seems original, even if on the surface it looks like something totally proprietary. You have to make sure that it is indeed proprietary and remains that way, and that you can go up against your competitors day in and day out by defining and redefining yourself, and them, in unequivocal terms.

Compete Against Yourself

One of the things that really drives me crazy is when some of the same people who think that the way to sell products is by

---

"While drawing . . . faint lines in the sand sounds nice in theory, in the real world, things aren't so neat and tidy. Somebody *is* going to compete with your products and try to steal your customers. If someone's going to do it, why shouldn't it be you?"

---

creating megabrands also say that you need to make sure that your brands don't overlap and compete with one another.

Along with megabrands, something else I don't believe in is portfolio management—that's when you build borders for each one of your brands, and no one brand can cross into the territory of the other brands in your portfolio. I just don't buy it. I believe that every brand has to fight against everybody else, even if everybody else is your own brand. That's the world as the consumer sees it, and that's the world that matters.

Portfolio management says that you create artificial categories for each of your products and you don't let any of them cross over into the others. Why? To avoid cannibalizing your own customer base. That's a great idea, and while drawing these faint lines in the sand sounds nice in theory, in the real world, things aren't so neat and tidy. Somebody *is* going to compete with your products and try to steal your customers. If someone's going to do it, why shouldn't it be you?

Look at what we did with Sprite in 1993. Sprite was always a lemon-lime drink competing in the lemon-lime category, and lemon-lime was a very easy section of the overall business to enter. The products were not very distinctive. They had been dominated by Sprite and 7UP, and the category really had never grown, except when there was the introduction of a new sweetener.

So we set out to broaden and reposition Sprite. What we said was, "Why don't we take it out of the lemon-lime category and make it compete in the overall beverage category." So we stopped talking about transparency and purity. Now, we told consumers, you shouldn't just think of Sprite when you want a lemon-lime drink, you should think of Sprite when you want to ally yourself with a brand that reflects your attitude about yourself and your life. That whole approach allowed us to position the brand differently in the marketplace and get it growing again.

This of course meant that we were putting it in competition with all of our other brands—including Coke and Diet Coke—but it was a good strategy. Sprite became the fastest growing soft drink in the world, and its volume tripled in four years to over a billion cases. Meanwhile we also aggressively positioned and marketed our other brands, and they grew as well. During this period the volume of the whole company grew by fifty percent, to fifteen billion cases a year from ten billion.

Because everything competes with everything else, I also believe in simultaneous marketing, not sequential marketing. By this, I mean that you should not schedule product tests so that they run one after another. The marketplace is never quiet, stable, or unchanging. You can't control what the economy or your competitors are going to do. So why should you try to run tests in controlled circumstances? When you have something new that you want to try out, you should just try it out, even if it means that you try many things in many places at the same time.

I think that if you put more balloons in the air, you'll figure out which ones are going to float. You need to do more programs on more brands at the same time. You can't believe the number of times that I have sat in meetings and somebody said, "February is the month for Coke, March is the month for Fanta, and Diet Coke will go in September." I said, "Well, why don't they all go in January." People would look at me like I was a nut, and say, "Well, we're going to cannibalize the system." I would say, "Well, the competition will cannibalize us if you don't do it that way."

Go simultaneous, don't go sequential. And it's okay to cannibalize your own brand, because it's better to eat your own babies than have a competitor do it. If for any reason your core brand has a weak spot and another brand is likely to take volume from that brand, you better go fix your core brand. Don't try to fix your problem by artificially protecting your core brand with portfolio management. Deal with your competition, internally and externally, by being competitive! After all, it's much better to lose volume to yourself than to your competitor.

Why Image Does Matter

Sometimes when I mouth off about how traditional marketers pay too much attention to creating images and not enough to selling stuff, people get the impression that I think image building is just a waste of time. Of course, that's totally wrong.

Marketers are making a big mistake when they hide behind the concept of building images so that they won't be held

"Too many marketers . . . don't really understand what branding and positioning need to do. So, the images they create are fuzzy, irrelevant, or boring."

accountable for producing any results. It's pure baloney, or worse, to suggest that marketing isn't about selling products and making money. But just because creating a positive image of your product in consumers' minds isn't the whole game doesn't mean that it's unimportant. It is very important, and you have to work at it aggressively.

Marketers who haven't made the connection between creating images and selling products often don't do a very good job at either of them. Obviously, lots of companies have created images that do a great job of helping to sell their products. Virgin Airways and the *Wall Street Journal* are just a couple of examples of products that have clear images that position them in potentially attractive spots in the consumers' universe of options. But too many marketers pay too much attention to the people in their ad agencies who talk about production values, WOW concepts, and winning awards, and they don't think enough about their objective and how the images they create are going to help or hurt them in achieving sales. They don't really understand what goes into branding and positioning, or what branding and positioning need to do. So, the images they create are fuzzy, irrelevant, or boring.

Again, it all starts with a strategy. You have to have a strategy about how you are going to dominate the market, and then you have to make sure that you create an image that helps you do it. If your strategy is high volume and low prices, then the image you want to create isn't going to be about luxury and choice. Southwest Airlines does not talk about food and comfort. On the other hand, if your strategy is to create an image like British Airways, which is to offer the most comfortable seats on every route you fly, then you do talk about pampering and you don't say too much about price. One ad campaign that I never could figure out was the Nissan campaign of a few years back. It showed an Asian guy with a dog. The pictures were interesting enough, but I still can't figure out what it was trying to communicate. Another campaign that I didn't get was the Delta Airlines "We love to fly and it shows" campaign that ran at a time when Delta was cutting costs and had really unhappy employees. The employees did not love their jobs. They hated their jobs, and it showed. Service was terrible, and the ads just highlighted that fact.

Even we at Coke weren't immune. Consider the "Have a Coke and smile" campaign that we ran when Pepsi was saying "Take the Pepsi Challenge and let your taste decide." Coke was focusing on image when Pepsi was going for the sales!

Those Nissan ads didn't work (according to press reports) because they weren't creating much of an image of Nissan, and they certainly weren't selling product. The Delta ads did create an image, but the image was contrary to what Delta was delivering at the time. Still other products have very clear images but are basically worthless because they don't stake out any position in the marketplace. The Milk Council is one of them. It has spent millions of dollars on the advertising campaign that shows celebrities with mustaches. I love the campaign. I have a great image of milk. It's a positive image, and I understand that milk isn't just for babies. But the image doesn't drive me to consumption because it hasn't positioned the product as having any desirable traits. And it's been running for six or seven years, and I haven't had a glass of milk in that whole time. A much better campaign would have given me reasons why I should drink more milk.

I also have a very clear image of Al Gore. It's a fairly positive image. I think he's probably a pretty nice guy. But there is nothing in that image that makes me particularly want to vote for him. That's because he doesn't have any strategy that I have yet discerned about staking out positions that would appeal to me.

How to Define Consumer Expectations That Your Competitor Can't Meet

The examples I just gave were mostly about using advertising to create an image for your product, but image is really the composite totality of everything that consumers know or think that

"Starbucks . . . has told me that good coffee doesn't come in vacuum-packed cans."

they know about your company and your product. I have an image that Volvos are very safe and boring cars. I have an image of Crest toothpaste that it is a reliable and effective product that I need. I have an image that my local grocery store is a great place to shop for tea bags, but I'm going to Starbucks for coffee.

How did I get these images in my mind? I got them in part from the advertising directed at me by the marketers for Volvos, Crest, and the local store. But I also got them from my experiences with their products, from my impressions of the people that I see using their products, from things that I have read and heard about the companies, and from their competitors.

One of the reasons that I think the local grocery store has lousy coffee is that Starbucks has told me so. It has trained me to expect something better, something different from what I can buy in the supermarket. Starbucks seized control of the dialogue in the marketplace for coffee and defined what is desirable in terms of price (high), form (beans), service (informed), and variety (many). Through its advertising, its stores, its chirpy but professional young workers, its lattes, cappuccinos, dark wooden counters, and fresh-roasted distribution system, it has told me that good coffee doesn't come in vacuum-packed cans. It has created not only an image for itself and its products, but also for everybody else in the coffee-selling business.

Starbucks has set the standards and redefined coffee drinking as an experience that it is singularly well prepared to provide.

For most people, image is a vaguely defined term that has something to do with feelings, or emotions, or subliminal impressions. It's one of those many things that marketers keep assuring us is indescribable and mystical. But like everything else in marketing, it is not only possible but essential that image building be done in a logical, strategic, and systematic manner.

In order to do that, you have to, again, think about it scientifically. You have to look at all the elements that go into creating images and then use them to build an overall image that is attractive and compelling to customers.

Know the Different Kinds of Imagery

The five elements of imagery that, in my experience, are most important are: trademark imagery, product imagery, associative

> **"Customers are going to have an image of your company and your product whether or not you consciously work to create one. . . .**
> **And that image is going to affect their decision about whether or not to buy."**

imagery, user imagery, and usage imagery. You have to use them together to build a coherent image.

Trademark Imagery

For Starbucks, the trademark identifiers are the green and black medallion, the color of the coffee bags, and the dark wood counters. The image that goes with these is that if you see them, you know that you are getting fresh-roasted, high-quality coffee. If you think of Kodak, the identifier of its trademark is the yellow box. Through years of experience and advertising, people have come to see Kodak's yellow packaging as signifying quality. It brings to mind quality film and quality paper, implying quality photographs, whether or not you're a great photographer. In the case of Disney, the trademark brings up Walt Disney, the theme parks, Mickey Mouse, Minnie Mouse, and family-focused, good clean fun.

These are things that form the essence, the core of a brand. They build over time and need to continue to build over time. They form the bank from which you withdraw when you want to either line extend or create additional products. Trademark imagery gives customers a level of confidence and continuity that gets them to listen to the next element of imagery. Trademark imagery is created over time, purposely appropriating for itself the images, actions, and events that shape what the trademark means to customers and potential customers.

Product Imagery

This is about the actual characteristics of the product. For Coke and Starbucks, it's the taste. For Diet Coke, it's the taste with only one calorie. For Kodak, it's the speed of the film and the quality of the pictures. For Disney, it's clean, wholesome, antiseptic entertainment. For British Airways, it's the comfort and safety of its flights. It is, in summary, what the product or service is supposed to do.

Associative Imagery

This is why sponsors sign up with sports teams to be the "Official Whatever It Is" of the NFL, the Atlanta Braves, or the Special Olympics. It's why Revlon hired Cindy Crawford and Pepsi teamed up with Michael Jackson. Associative imagery is an effort to find common ground with consumers and say to them, "I like what you like. Our interests are your interests, and by the way, I have something else here that you should be interested in." It's a valuable part of the mix of reasons that you give consumers to buy your product, but it cannot stand alone. In its deals with baseball and the NFL, Fox TV is using associative imagery to answer the question: Is this a real network? Of course it must be, if it has the NFL and major league baseball. Associative imagery is what I call borrowed interest because it borrows the consumers' interest in something else to get them interested in your product.

Although the connections are not always instantly clear, associative imagery, like the other elements of marketing, has to stem from and be grounded in strategy. It is foolish to sponsor something that does not fit with the overall strategy of the brand. Why does Coke sponsor soccer? Because its base of consumers identify with the sport and by sponsoring soccer it is putting its brands and its messages in fertile ground. Consumers identify with the sport and they listen to what you have to say more openly. Think of Revlon and models, Budweiser and racing. You should only associate yourself with something if you have a strategy and a reason for doing it, not because your competition is. Pepsi's choice to ally with Michael Jackson, and then Lionel Richie, didn't sway Coke to do the same thing, and for good reason.

User Imagery

User imagery is about what kind of people like and use your product. The goal here is to make consumers look at your advertising and think, "Hey, those people in those commercials or those print ads are people like me. They are people I like and people I'd like to be like. If they're using that product or service, then that is an endorsement and confirmation that I should use the product as well." It's why ads for megavitamins and nutritional supplements show old people who are swimming and kayaking and dancing and kissing. It's why models are always young and thin and beautiful.

Usage Imagery

How and is the product consumed? In a bar? In a home? In a restaurant? Is it used by businesspeople? What is it and how is it used? And may I suggest some new uses for you? Depending on the audience, there is tremendous variation in usage imagery. In Mexico, Coca-Cola is considered a part of lunch; in fact, it usually is consumed with most foods. Food without Coca-Cola is almost like an incomplete meal. But this is not necessarily true in Japan, Ireland, or other places. Different messages work in different places, so there isn't one usage image that is going to be relevant everywhere.

The proper mixing of these image elements is actually what creates the image of a brand. The advertising process has to build, maximize, capitalize, and exploit each one of the strengths and weaknesses of each image element in order to make sure that the brand gets vested on an ongoing basis with more and more elements.

It's important to remember that customers are going to have an image of your company and your product whether or not you consciously work to create one. Your packaging, your distribution outlets, the rudeness or politeness of the people answering your telephones, everything that a consumer sees or hears about your company is going to create that image. And that image is going to affect their decision about whether or not to buy.

Stake Out Your Turf

So, what's the difference between image and position? A brand's image is the overall impression that people have about it. Its position is what the marketers want people to think and feel about it. As I've said, I have an image that Volvos are safe and

"The reason that Southwest Airlines is so popular is that it does a very good job of underpromising and overdelivering."

boring and that Al Gore is nice and boring. The people marketing Volvo and Al Gore had something to do with creating those
images. In Volvo's case, the company's marketers have positioned the brand in the marketplace as being a rugged, reliable
family car that is safer than most others. In Al Gore's case, he
and his marketers have failed to stake out a strong position, so I
have developed an image that he is bland.

Deciding exactly what positions you are going to stake out
and what it is that you are going to promise is critical. There is a
formula that my good friend and colleague Scott Miller and I
developed a long time ago, which we used to call D.A.D. and
we later changed to D.O.C.S. The first one stood for **D**efine and
Deliver. It evolved into **D**efine, **O**verdeliver, **C**laim (that is, make
sure that everyone hears about the overdelivery), and this will
give you **S**uccess.

The reason that Southwest Airlines is so popular is that it
does a very good job of underpromising and overdelivering.
The people at Southwest have engineered a consumer offering
for an airline that bypasses many of the problems that airlines
have in delivering on promises. How many times have you seen
a commercial where a beautiful flight attendant serves you din-
ner on fine china, and the announcer talks about the fact that
you, in addition to a great (safe, on-time) flight, will enjoy a
wonderful dining experience—only to get on the airplane to
find out that they are out of chicken, the wine selection is prac-
tically nonexistent, and the flight attendants are certainly not
those you saw in the commercials?

Southwest has solved the problem by promising customers
very little. More importantly, it is a promise that Southwest can
deliver every time. Southwest says that if you get to the airport
early, you will get on the plane first. It so happens that there are
three rows of seats on either side of the plane, which means
that if you are in the first third of customers to arrive, you will
sit on the aisle, if you choose to. If you arrive at the airport in
the second third, then you get the second chance to board the
plane, which means you will get the window seat if all of the
aisle seats are taken. If you get there last, you will get on and sit

in whatever seat is left. There is very little chance that you will be disappointed once you know what the boarding process is and what's expected. You won't be looking for a window seat if you get on the plane at the last minute, and actually you might be pretty happy if you found one.

The second thing is that they don't promise you any food. They give you a bag of peanuts and a Coke, and usually that is pretty hard to screw up. Lastly, they promise that they will take you from place to place at reasonable prices, and they do. They set up a pretty broad offering that satisfies lots of airline flyers, and they deliver every single time. The big airlines, the other guys, usually don't. They promise luxury and you get the cattle car.

Consciously define the expectation as something that you can deliver. Even better, define it as something that you can overdeliver, and once you overdeliver, make sure that you proclaim to the world the fact that you did.

Don't Fight the Brand Immune System

It's almost always good to broaden your position and to expand your promises as your ability to deliver improves. When you

"New Coke represented a foreign organism to consumers and the immune system sent antibodies to get rid of it."

figure out how to do something, especially if it's something that you think your competitor can't do, you should make that a promise and hope that consumers will begin to make it a nonnegotiable demand. There are, however, limits beyond which consumers won't let you go. I call the forces that set these limits a brand's immune system.

There are some elements that the immune system will just not let you introduce, no matter how brilliantly and diligently you work.

This was one of the many valuable lessons that we learned from New Coke. After we had recovered from the unexpectedly harsh public response to New Coke and regained our momentum in marketing Classic Coke, we went back and asked ourselves: So, exactly what happened, and why did it happen? One of the answers that we came up with was that we had run into the immune system of the brand Coca-Cola. In other words, we discovered that in the public's eyes, Coke's fundamental core was continuity and stability. What New Coke was promising was choice and change. This meant that the consumers who had a strong understanding and feeling for the brand and its core foundational elements would not accept something that seemed so contrary to what they understood the product to be about. New Coke represented a foreign organism to consumers and the immune system sent antibodies to get rid of it.

While Coke stands for continuity and stability, Pepsi on the other hand, does stand for choice and change. Its positioning has always been about youth, doing things differently and unpredictably. Pepsi is the insurgent, not the incumbent, but this has its limitations as well. For Coke, a sentimental ad about going to a family reunion and warm fuzzy images of Santa Claus drinking Coke might be perfect, whereas for Pepsi drinkers, ads like this would be a major shock. Managing these limitations is very critical.

Even though a brand's immune system will often limit the things that you can do with it, understanding the immune system can allow you some freedom. That's because the immune system provides a good, clear alarm for what will work and what won't. You can freely try all sorts of things when you know that the system will let you know when you screw up. All you have to do is keep your eyes open and be willing to accept the message when you get it. If you do something that violates the immune system, you can be sure that the brand will start acting up.

In extreme cases, like New Coke, sales will go to hell, or the consumers will throw fits, and you can fix the problem immediately. But sometimes the changes are more subtle. If you diligently do your research, however, and you see the drivers of consumption changing, that's a warning sign. If the drivers are changing because consumers are adding reasons to buy your product, then that's probably good. But if you are losing some of the old drivers, you could be in big trouble, and if you don't act quickly, you could kill the brand.

Can you imagine a Close-Up toothpaste with baking soda? I can't. The whole premise of Close-Up is that it is a transparent gel with mouthwash. If you add abrasives, you lose the fundamental product. How about a low-priced version of Chivas Regal? A General Motors bicycle? Or Nike dress shoes? Those may be far-fetched examples, but they make the point. Premium pricing is a central Chivas Regal trait. General Motors is about things with motors, and Nike's promise is athletic performance, not formal wear.

Control the Dialogue

More important than managing limitations is controlling the overall dialogue in the marketplace as defined by all of the par-

"Positioning the competition means defining the rules of the game in the marketplace."

ticipants. So far, Al Gore is fortunate, because his potential rivals have not positioned him as standing for something that voters won't like. But if he stays in the race, he will soon have a position whether he likes it or not.

Either you choose the territory in the competitive marketplace that you want to occupy, or your competitors will do it for you.

Pepsi positioned Coke many years ago. They started at "Twice as much for a nickel too," and they based their positioning on saying, "Hey look, Coke is too expensive. It doesn't give you as much product for the same money." In this way, they bought positioning for themselves and positioned the competition as well.

Consciously positioning the competition in the marketplace is one of the most effective marketing lessons of the last fifty years. Pepsi was quite masterful at this, and they did this for years until the early 1990s, when Coke finally decided not to let them keep doing it. After the "Twice as much for a nickel too" campaign, Pepsi went to "You've got a lot to live and Pepsi's got a lot to give," which then transformed itself into the Pepsi Generation. Both of these positioned Coke as being for old and stodgy people and Pepsi for the young and vigorous. In the late 1970s, they faltered a bit. Then this little agency in Dallas came up with a great campaign: "Take the Pepsi Challenge. Let your taste decide," it said as it showed confirmed Coca-Cola drinkers expressing surprise that they liked the taste of Pepsi better.

Positioning the competition means defining the rules of the game in the marketplace. Airlines do this a lot when they keep changing the definition of what a good flight or a good value is. Not only is the Southwest experience an important one, but also look at what Virgin is doing. It constantly refreshes and changes its positioning, redefining its competitors on terms consumers never dreamed of. Did it occur to you before Virgin to expect a massage, manicure, or pedicure in the sky? It hadn't crossed my mind, but now I want it.

Ronald Reagan did this in unequivocal terms when he defeated Jimmy Carter by saying, "America, are you better off right now than you were four years ago?" He set this as the test at a time when it was obvious that Americans were in the midst of a malaise and were not feeling well off at all. He did this further by saying, "Here you go again, Jimmy," labeling Carter as a man who had no new ideas and was not providing solutions.

In 1992, Bill Clinton defined the dialogue on the basis of the economy. George Bush thought that Ronald Reagan and he had already fixed the economy, so he was trying to broaden his appeal by talking about other things. But Clinton, with the help of James Carville, noted that there were still many middle-class Americans feeling squeezed. So they coined the slogan that "It's the economy, stupid," meaning if you're not in good shape, if your family is not in good shape, there has to be change. All of the experts say that this is how Clinton won the election in 1992.

Limit the Issues but Broaden the Dialogue

In addition to making a straight, head-on offensive, both Pepsi and Clinton also did something else very important, which was to

> **"Whenever possible, narrow how your competitor is defined to a single trait or quality while simultaneously broadening yours."**

narrow the positioning of the opponent. In the cola wars, Pepsi narrowed Coke to the single issue of taste. What Pepsi did with the Pepsi Challenge was to say that none of the elements that consumers associated with Coke—namely its history, emotion, constancy and stability—mattered because the only issue was taste. Clinton, in effect, said that it didn't matter what else George Bush had to say if you weren't happy with your own finances.

This is a key concept: whenever possible, narrow how your competitor is defined to a single trait or quality while simultaneously broadening yours.

Compare for a Strategic Advantage

The Pepsi Challenge is also a good example of an extremely effective type of advertising that I think marketers should use a lot more of. This is positive comparative advertising. When most people think of comparative advertising they think of the nega-

"If I tell you that my airline is very safe because we have lots of full-time mechanics who perform a gazillion tests every day on every plane, you are going to start wondering about the other guys."

tive stuff, and that's why, for the most part, they shy away from it. Short-term negative ads do work, which is why desperate politicians start mudslinging as election day gets closer. But over the long haul, negative ads don't build any loyalty because all they say about your product is that it isn't as bad as the other guy's. Pointing out, or even asserting, that your opponent in this election is a lying, cheating, crook may get you votes. Or maybe not, if you haven't given anyone any positive reasons to like you. So where does that put you next year, when your opponent is an honorable, decent person? If anything, it puts you in a hole because negative ads can really irritate consumers who don't want to be associated with mud throwers.

By contrast, positive comparative advertising is not only a good idea; it is also one that marketers must increasingly embrace because it does three very important things at once. It positions you or your product as having valuable traits; it helps you control the dialogue in the market by defining the standards for judgment; and it narrows the position of your competition to an area where it is weaker than you are. In the case of the Pepsi Challenge, Pepsi directly named Coke as the competitor, but it didn't actually say, or really even imply, that there was anything wrong with Coke. It didn't say that Coke is a lousy, inferior product that doesn't satisfy your thirst, is filled with chemicals, and tastes like dirt. All it said explicitly was that "some people who like Coke have discovered that they think Pepsi tastes better. Try it for yourself." In other words, taste is the test, and Pepsi tastes good.

While Pepsi named Coke, naming the competitor isn't what's important in comparative marketing. The thing that matters is that you establish a standard for judging, and then you clearly show how well your product meets or exceeds the standard. Once the consumer buys into the standard, he or she will make the comparison. If I tell you that my airline is very safe because we have lots of full-time mechanics who perform a gazillion tests every day on every plane, you are going to start wondering about the other guys. I don't need to name them for you. I can establish difference by stating what I do without ever mentioning the competitor, and you will do the rest.

Steal from the Competition

Take another look at Sprite, and you can see how important positioning is.

> **"We saw this as an opportunity to compete with Pepsi in some of its markets by stepping on their positioning of choice and change."**

Sprite was born somewhat haphazardly many years ago, when the Coca-Cola Company found itself with a lot of extra production capacity. Lemon-lime was not a category in which we had a presence, so some smart guy said, "Hey, why don't we produce a lemon-lime product in order to enter that market?" The company at this time had a little mascot, an animated television character called Sprite, that was used in Coke ads. He was a peppy, little guy with a crown on his head, so Coke decided to start making Sprite, the soft drink. Unfortunately, the company didn't have any strategy or do any positioning for the brand. It just said, "Here's Sprite. It's clear and it's a lemon-lime."

As a result, for years and years, Sprite swam in a pool of sameness with the other lemon-limes. The definition of lemon-limes was cheap lemonade, and all over the world, consumers drank the lemonades only once in a long while. Occasionally, the two major players in the category tried to change the whole category. Do you remember the Un-Cola by 7UP, which tried to position the category as a product you drank when you were looking for a change of pace? The problem with a change-of-pace drink is that you only drink it when you want a change of pace, and there is not enough volume to make you any money. 7UP again was innovative when it introduced the no-caffeine, no-preservatives campaign. The business actually grew, and this triggered the caffeine-free colas—Tab, Diet Coke, Coke, and the Pepsis. But it didn't grow a lot, and Sprite didn't either.

I firmly believe that unless you have a hundred percent of the market, you can always grow by stealing customers from the competition. But Sprite had done no positioning to differentiate itself from 7UP, so it was stuck with the slow growth rate of the overall market.

In 1992, I was hired as a consultant by Sunny Burrows, the brand manager of Coca-Cola USA, a division of The Coca-Cola Company. She wanted me to help her figure out what was wrong with Sprite. What we learned gave us the idea to position Sprite not as a lemon-lime but as a drink with an attitude. In the course of our research, we interviewed both heavy users of Sprite and light or dual users to find out what they thought about Sprite. Our plan was to start a debate so we could hear what happened when we asked the heavy users to defend their Sprite against the unenthusiastic light users, and to see if we could use the statements of the heavy users to move the light users.

The interesting thing that we learned from both types of consumers was that they didn't much care at all that Sprite was a lemon-lime drink. What they liked about it was that it had attitude, it reflected their own attitude, which was a bit cheeky or unconventional. We saw this as an opportunity to compete with Pepsi in some of its markets by stepping on their positioning of choice and change. We recommended that Sprite ignore its lemon-lime roots, that it ignore the clarity positioning and move out of the lemon-lime category and into the general beverage market. Our recommendation was so well received at the time that the project was shelved.

Soon after that, Coca-Cola's president, Doug Ivester, asked me to come back to the company. On the first day I showed up, I called and asked, "Whatever happened with that Sprite project we did a year ago?" The new brand manager on Sprite said, "Well, we're kind of thinking about it." So I said, "Let's do it." We told the ad agency that we wanted to position the brand outside the lemon-lime category and more in the Pepsi arena, and they came up with the "Follow your instincts. Obey your thirst" campaign. Redefining the rules in these terms made Sprite the fastest growing brand for the last six years. Its volume tripled to over one billion cases in a business that had been flat for years and years.

To reinforce the new positioning, we made a deal with the National Basketball Association. Basketball has a gutsy image, and that is exactly what we wanted for Sprite. Before that, the only brands that had big campaigns and associations with major sport were the big boys, the Cokes and Pepsis, but never a little brand like Sprite. At the time the company was in negotiations with the NBA, everyone was thinking that the association would be with the brand Coca-Cola. So I went and talked to David Stern, the commissioner of the NBA, and I explained to him that brand Coca-Cola did not have the resources to stand behind all sports, as it was already overextended with affiliations to over 20 other sports, so it couldn't take on all the activities and events that were associated with the NBA. But I said that Sprite could do it, and that we could spend a lot of money promoting both the NBA and the brand. David saw the benefits for both the NBA and Sprite and agreed to it with a handshake. Today, Sprite is very clearly associated with basketball and with the attitude of basketball. This is the kind of associative imagery that works because the two partners stand for the same traits in the consumers' minds. It's all part of a single positioning strategy.

Advertising is just a piece of what makes a brand and gives it a position and an image. Everything that a company does, from promotions to packaging design to distribution, washes over its brands. So, always remember: everything communicates. Every brand has to have a positioning strategy, and everything you do with regard to that brand must communicate it.

5

WHAT DO BILL CLINTON, PRINCESS DI, AND RAMADAN HAVE TO DO WITH SELLING STUFF?

To be successful, marketing has to be focused on consumers. Everyone knows that, right? But what everyone doesn't know is that it's not enough to be obsessed with your consumer in a vacuum. People don't live in isolation; everything they see, feel, do, and think affects how they buy. What most marketers don't pay enough attention to is what's going on in the world and how it's *affecting* consumers.

If you asked them, most marketers would say, "Sure, I know what's going on in the world. I'm highly educated, well connected, I watch CNN, and I read the newspaper every day." Well, that may be so, but most of them don't spend five minutes a week thinking about how the merger of Travelers and Citicorp or the change in Republican party leadership is going to affect their customers' behaviors. They may think about obvious things like the fact that a slump in the stock market isn't going to be great for selling yachts and vacation homes. And it may prompt some companies to cut ad budgets—which is stupid, because precisely when you need to raise them is when customers don't seem in the mood to buy (you need to give them a reason to).

The truth is that *everything* that happens impacts everything else. Everything is interconnected, and as such, everything that is happening in your consumer's world matters to you! Consumers live in an ocean of information where the movement of each molecule affects all the others, and a good marketer should be like a whale swimming though the ocean, filtering for food in the water around it.

Why do fans tear down goalposts at the end of football games? Why is body piercing so popular with the under-thirty crowd? Why do people cruise in the left-hand lane on the highway? Why don't more Americans vote? What do these questions have to do with selling soft drinks, lightbulbs, or airline tickets?

I don't really know the answers to the first four questions, but I do know that it is my job to ask them. And that it's also yours. That's because people do things for reasons. It's our job as marketers and as businesspeople to figure out what those reasons are and how to apply them to our businesses. All of their actions rise out of and reflect their emotions, opinions, and circumstances. Whether it's tearing down goalposts, piercing their tongues, cruising in the left-hand lane, not voting, or buying or not buying soft drinks, lightbulbs, or airline tickets, it's all related. I watch TV to find out what other good marketing and businesspeople are doing. But I also watch and think about the number of voters that vote in an election, the trends in restaurants, people's behavior in the sports stadium, in the piercing parlor, on the highway, and in the voting booth. By looking at and analyzing consumers, we can learn things that will help get them into the store or on the telephone to buy our products. You've got to look everywhere and learn everywhere, because everything is connected.

You Can Never Know Too Much about Consumers

The notion that you need to study consumer behavior is not revolutionary. Marketers have always watched consumers and asked questions, but what most marketers don't do is watch consumers *closely* enough—and then think about the implications of what they've observed. Consumers are not just one link in a value chain that also includes manufacturing, distribution, planning, purchasing, and sales. They are not just "one of the

"If you ignore a single bit of potentially valuable information about (consumers), you are wasting money."

things" that marketers have to think about. They are not even the first among equals on the list of things that marketers have to think about.

They are, quite possibly, the only thing worth thinking about. Everything else—including the all-important strategy—comes second to your consumers.

During the 1992 presidential election, James Carville became famous for constantly reminding Candidate Clinton that the most important issue that people cared about was their finances. "It's the economy, stupid" became the watch phrase of the campaign and a verbal model used by people everywhere. My version for marketers is: "It's the consumers, stupid." If you are in business and your goal is to maximize profits, as it should be, the only way you can succeed is by focusing on, understanding, and pleasing consumers. If you don't do that, you will never be able to succeed.

I know—you have to think about others things too. You have to have salespeople, and a distribution system. You have to have efficient manufacturing, cost-effective purchasing, and good relations with the middle people who get your product into consumers' hands. But the ultimate issue is *who is going to buy your stuff?* Who is going to fly on your airline? Who is going to drive your car? Who is going to drink your beer? Who is going to wash their clothes with your detergent? It's the consumer, stupid! All of those other constituencies are meaningless without them.

At the heart of marketing, at the heart of business, are the people who actually shell out the money to buy your product or service. You have to constantly think about them and study them and build everything you do around them. I can't emphasize this point strongly enough, so let me say it again: *everything that happens to consumers and everything that consumers do should affect your marketing decisions. If you ignore a single bit of potentially valuable information about them, you are wasting money.*

When I say that you have to study and think about consumers, I don't mean in the old-fashioned way that most marketers think about consumers. Sure, it's important to look at buying patterns and how consumers relate to your products and to the ones that they compete with. If you are selling apple juice, of course, it's a good idea to look at how often and why people buy orange juice and Diet Coke and even fresh fruit. But to really connect with them, to get them to stop buying something else and to start buying your product, you need to look a lot deeper and a lot more broadly.

You have to understand—or if not understand to at least try to understand—the whole environment in which people live. Anything that happens in that environment is going to change what consumers do and don't do. Economic conditions will change people's mind-set. Climate changes, a hurricane, a major event, the death of a public figure, an election—whatever it is, it is going to change how consumers think and will have an influence on how they think about your product. This means that you have to look at politics, economics, history, social trends, fads, fears, and entertainment. And you have to think about it real hard. Just as buying behavior doesn't happen in isolation, neither does consumer behavior.

Watch the World, Not Just Your Market

When you are selling mass-market products, you can't interview all of your potential customers to find out what they want. But, fortunately, you don't have to. There is plenty of information out there that will tell you what consumers are thinking and feeling. Unfortunately, most marketers don't use it, because they

"We took our lead from (Tony) Blair and changed our advertising and promotions, and it worked for us as well."

don't fully appreciate how broadly marketers need to think and how events and situations that seem far removed from their product will affect their ability to sell.

A standard operating procedure for me at Coca-Cola was that every time there was an election in a country, I would ask our people to hire the pollsters who had worked for the new president or prime minister. I figured that he or she knew more about what was going on in the mind-sets of people than anybody else, and I wanted our people to have that information so that we could use it to refine our marketing. When Tony Blair was elected in Britain, for example, the analysts and pollsters pointed out that he did so on a very thin platform that promised change but had few specifics. His pitch was basically, "Look, it's time for a change. My government will be different." That doesn't seem like much for the British people to go on, but it worked for him. He won the election. So when we asked ourselves what this said about the British public, we concluded that people were tired of the status quo and would be interested in something, anything, different.

We took our lead from Blair and changed our advertising and promotions, and it worked for us as well. We didn't reposition the product or really change any of our promises. We just started doing different things. We began speaking more directly to the consumers through things such as contour bottles, sponsorships, and a barrage of consumer promotions, and we directed fewer of our efforts toward trade promotions and other activities that focused on the retailers. Coke sales, which had been basically flat in Britain, began to climb again. To outside observers, it may have appeared that we were just behaving like old-style marketers and changing for the sake of change. But the truth is that, yes, we were changing for the sake of reexplaining our brands, but we were doing it because the public had indicated that that's what it wanted. This is a key difference between old-style marketing and marketing that emphasizes the point that I am making throughout this book. Marketing is not a mysterious art based on intuition and whim. It is a science based on research and information.

The death of Princess Diana was also a very telling event. Here was a woman who had been publicly portrayed as neurotic, and roundly criticized for going on television to talk about her illicit sex life. And yet millions of people around the world were completely overwrought over her death. As I watched the wailing and mourning crowds on TV in fascination, I said to myself, "Something big is going on here."

But I didn't leave it at that. I was convinced there was something in the reaction to her death that we at Coke could learn from. So we quickly launched a research project to try and understand what was going on. What we found was the reason that people connected to Diana was that her life had been filled with extremes, but she had somehow pulled them together. She was a fabulously wealthy playgirl, but she was also a good mother. When she wasn't hanging out on the yachts of jet-setters, she was devoting herself to serious causes such as eliminating land mines and helping child welfare. She was a gorgeous woman, but she had many of the same problems as everyone else. Yet what we came to understand was that she represented in people's minds a balance of the good and the bad in all of us.

People were mourning the loss of a role model. Sure, she was richer, more privileged, and more beautiful than most of us, but that wasn't the point. What we learned was that she was an icon of survival for millions of people. She gave hope to other people who were struggling with the conflicts in their lives.

As a result of this exercise, we didn't do anything dramatic.

We didn't put together advertising or promotions that tried to take advantage of Diana or her death, we didn't run big ads that said: "Drown your sorrows in Coca-Cola." But we did learn a lot from this exercise. And we adjusted our mix of ads to send a balance of basic messages, ones that celebrated life and ones that suggested comfort and dependability. The changes we made were subtle, but the important thing was that we were looking, and listening, and learning, and then acting.

And it worked.

The Rise of Consumer Democracy

There has been a seismic change in consumer markets in the past two decades that I think many people have missed. This is

"Consumers understand that they have a choice. . . . but they have no idea how to decide."

the rise of what I call "consumer democracy." What I mean by this is that suddenly, thanks to a variety of factors, most notably technology and the development of global markets, consumers have more choices than ever before.

This development is probably the most obvious in Eastern Europe and Asia. The decline of communism and the opening of free markets have clearly increased choices for consumers. Even in countries where the economies have crashed, people still have far more options than before in terms of how they are going to allocate their limited resources. And in developing countries, infrastructures and distribution have improved, so that a lot more products have become available in the stores. As a result, choice has become an important element in markets where just a few years ago no choices were available.

At the same time, great change has also occurred in more

democratic and industrialized economies. In part, this is the result of technology and what the economists call commoditization. As one company comes up with a unique product, all of its competitors have the ability to very quickly imitate it. So consumers end up with a huge array of basically identical products, or interchangeable commodities. Also, with the proliferation of cable TV channels, the growth of the Internet, and a seemingly endless supply of products and activities available in all shapes and sizes at all hours of the day and night, people in industrial societies have come to expect and demand an endless variety of consumer products—and more information about these products than was ever before available.

These developments have enormous implications for marketers in that they present both a huge challenge and a huge opportunity. The challenge is that there is a lot more competition, so marketers have to work harder to make sure that consumers choose their products. The opportunity is in the fact that when customers have choices, they have to make decisions. And in order to make those decisions, they need information.

I think that one of the main reasons that only thirty-four percent of the people in the United States voted in the 1998 elections was that the other sixty-six percent didn't know who to vote for, or didn't care which candidate won because no one had given them enough information or enough reason to vote one way or the other. They had the option of choosing but no compelling reasons for doing so.

The same thing is increasingly happening in the marketplace. Consumers understand that they have a choice. They understand that there are many things out there that they can choose from in each category, but they have no idea how to decide. How do you buy gas in today's environment? Do you really understand octane and how much detergent the gasoline has to have in order to clean the engine? I don't. How do you buy a car—based on size (small, medium, or large)? Almost all cars now offer front-wheel drive, automatic braking systems, cruise control, tinted windows, power windows and locks, and on and on and on. So which one do you buy?

And how about blue jeans? It isn't very hard to get into the blue jeans business. All you need to know is who the manufacturers are over in the Far East and where to buy the denim, and you can get the jeans made and on the market in no time flat. So then consumers are looking at a seemingly generic pair of jeans that happens to have your brand on it, but there's no reason to buy yours versus anyone else's. They don't know whether the denim should be thick or thin, they don't know whether the jeans should have riveted edges or five pockets. Somebody has to tell them, and that somebody is you.

Don't Let Price Be the Tiebreaker

If you don't tell consumers how to choose, they are either not going to choose, or they are going to choose based on the one

> **"Even if your product isn't that different, better, or special, it's the job of the marketer to make people think that it's different, better, and special."**

thing they do understand: price. Of course, if price is the predominant element in the choices that your customers make, your profitability and the health of your business will go into the tank pretty quickly. So you need to give them other bases for deciding to buy your product. In a free-market society, consumers sit around looking at one another with glassy eyes, listening to the things we say as manufacturers or purveyors of services and goods, and they ask us, "Why should I buy your product?" The challenge and opportunity for marketers is to tell them.

The car companies actually do this very well. Price and

styling don't really narrow the field very much, so they tell us about all sorts of other things. They teach us about rack-and-pinion steering, twenty-five-inch wheels, ABS brakes, and all kinds of other things. Again, most of these things don't matter much to us, like the torque, the width of the wheels, the mileage per gallon, and the speed at which you can go from zero to sixty—especially today, when most of the time you are in your car you are in traffic where you can only drive twenty-five miles per hour. Nevertheless, car companies are trying to give us concrete reasons to buy their cars. And the company that gives the consumers the most appealing reasons is the one that will get the sales.

In the old days, you didn't need to explain this much because there weren't that many choices. Today, and in the future, you need to tell consumers why they should buy, and you need to tell them why they should buy your stuff—every day. This means that you need to sell to them in your packaging, your shelf talkers, your point of sale, your advertising, how your trucks are painted. You need to tell them more and more and more about why your product is different. There are more and more and more of the same products, and therefore there is more and more of a need to differentiate not only on the basis of intrinsics, but also on the basis of extrinsics. The intrinsics are the actual benefits of the products, whether it has an enzyme, or it has more sugar, or it has more of a kick, or it has a vitamin. Extrinsics are all of the associative imagery, trademark, usage, and user imagery that I talked about in chapter 4. Even if your product *isn't* that different, better, or special, it's the job of the marketer to make people *think* that it's different, better, and special.

Consumer Communism—It's the Pits

If you don't connect with customers and with persuasive marketing, what you will get is consumer communism. That's when people just start buying whatever everybody else buying. They will listen to the last message they've heard or what their aunt,

"They will listen to the last message they've heard or what their aunt, husband, or wife says or thinks."

husband, or wife says or thinks. They recognize that they don't really have the knowledge to choose, so they decide to do what everyone else is doing. If it's good enough for them, they think, it must be good enough for me. Consumer communism is pretty scary stuff and very bad news for marketers because it means consumers are listening to somebody else, and not you.

I looked into buying a time-share of a plane a while ago, and there were three options: I could buy a piece of a Hawker, a Learjet, or a Citation. I spent endless days and months trying to sort out what the differences were, and everybody kept on telling me that all of the planes were about the same. They all had the same avionics. They are all pretty safe. They have all the systems, they have stabilizers, and they are all comfortable. I was desperate and couldn't figure out which one to buy. I talked to the companies, and they weren't explaining to me why I should buy one or the other. I eventually started thinking about price, which is the ultimate tiebreaker. Price is the one that you use when you have no other ideas about why you should buy a service or a product.

Eventually, for me, price did not turn out to be the deciding factor, and I did not fall into the consumer communism trap of just listening to my friends. But I did something else that is just as dangerous for marketers, which is that I came up with my own criteria. Because the companies didn't give me any way to choose, I developed my own list of desirable attributes without their input. For me, they were range and flexibility of scheduling. And when I found out that some of the planes didn't have as much of a range as the others and that the flexibility of one was better, that is how I made the decision.

If the airplane marketers had been really doing their job, I wouldn't have had to work so hard. If they had really been thinking about their potential customers, they would have known what mattered to customers like me and then they would have made the sale by talking about that. In a sense, it was a matter of the old "features and benefits" issue. They talked about the features of the airplanes like the air-to-ground systems and the fact that the plane sat 7, when what I really cared about were the benefits. Were their planes and services going to take me where I wanted to go, when I wanted to go, safely and in a manner that I thought was convenient? In my case, I thought that all three of the companies that I was talking to made safe planes, so convenience was the issue. Since the market for private-jet time-shares is pretty small, in this instance, the best way to find out what mattered to me in terms of convenience would have been to ask me. If they had, they would have found out that I am a person who for many years has traveled literally millions of miles a year. I like to travel for pleasure, and my work demands that I travel. But I hate the hassles associated with airports and flying. I want to go where I want to go, when I want to go. I am willing to pay for that service, but in return, I want a company that has enough planes, with the range and flexibility to fly the distances I want to fly and to change schedules quickly.

The mistake that the plane marketers made was in thinking about themselves and their product and not thinking about me, the customer.

If People Are Fasting during the Day, Sell to Them at Night

As products become more global, marketers will increasingly have to take into account cultures and values that may be different from their own. I think that I may have been helped on this score a bit by the fact that I am a Mexican who has worked for American companies all of my life. But even so, it has been a learning process. By now it seems obvious, but I remember a

"Sales declines didn't reflect reduced consumption . . . but rather reduced availability."

few years back when someone at Coke presented me with a sales projection that showed sales in the Mideast would decline sharply in January from the year before. The person presenting the plan explained that most of the Moslem fasting period of Ramadan would fall in January, meaning that during this month-long period Moslems can't eat or drink anything from dawn to dusk. Because of the difference in the lunar calendar, the date changes, and this particular year, January would be our slow month.

At first, it seemed to make sense. When millions of people are fasting, it is easy to assume that consumption of food and drink in the areas where they live is going to fall. But that's lazy thinking. The fact is that Moslems don't stop eating and drinking during Ramadan; they just stop doing it *during the day.*

Sales declines didn't reflect reduced consumption of beverages, but rather reduced availability because stores and restaurants were closed at night when people were eager to drink and open during the day, when shoppers could only think about eating and drinking later. Further, the fact that our advertising was directed at people who were awake and thirsty during the day and yet unable to buy our products, meant that much of our daytime advertising was being wasted on an unreceptive audience.

If you're fasting and can't drink during the day, the last thing you want to see is a nice, inviting ad about how refreshing a Coke would be.

We realized that if we wanted to sell soft drinks during Ramadan, we needed to do it at night. Even if people were going to the store during the day to stock up for the night, they were still going to be a lot more enthusiastic if we recognized that. So we changed our advertising and then ran promotions and activities that would allow us to sell product during those times. We were careful not to try to take commercial advantage of this very important holiday, while at the same time addressing the real need that people had to eat and drink after fasting. We just did what we could to make Coke products a part of breaking the fast. Since there are 1.2 billion Moslems in the world, even a tiny increase in sales can make a significant difference.

When One Thing Changes, Everything Changes

The fundamental thing that you must remember and remember well is that when the environment changes, consumers change.

> **"The political upheavals and uncertainty in the United States have made people more cautious and economically conservative."**

It boggles my mind to think that marketers all over the world don't factor political movements or social changes into their plans. It is not that consumers necessarily have faith in the economy or the government; but the world is made up of molecules, and when there is a significant change in the arrangement of those molecules, all of them get jolted.

Of course, everybody talks about the weather and the economy. Those are easy things to talk about, but what happens in a country like Korea where the economy tanks, and all of a sudden the psyche of the people gets jolted? Stability is no longer the rule. Everyone is living in chaos. What happens when there's a major swing in politics from the right to the left or from the left to the right?

Think about a glass of water that is already three-quarters full, and you fill it up to the top. The quarter that you just put in doesn't sit on top; it actually blends and mixes with the rest of the molecules of the glass. The same thing happens to an environment as a whole, as well as to a specific marketplace. Anytime something new gets thrown in, it changes how each one of the molecules sits, how one relates to another. It is critically important to remember this to stay ahead of the curve.

I am a firm believer that the events of the last year relating to President Clinton had a deep effect on how Americans feel about everything. I believe that it has affected the consumer's psyche with regard to their purchases and with regard to how they view their future, and how they relate to self-indulgence, savings, going to see someone they haven't seen in a long time, or having a family reunion. My own personal belief is that the political upheavals and uncertainty in the United States have made people more cautious and economically conservative and more aware of the things that they have in their lives that they value. I think that this is having an effect on everything from their willingness to buy a new house or a car, to an increased desire to stay home, visit friends, and hold family reunions. I also think that my belief that uncertainty brings conservatism has been borne out by public behavior. I read in February that the turnover in stocks in the current stock market is very high, close to 1929, the year of the crash. I have to believe that all of these issues and the issues affecting the American people have a strong influence on how the markets are behaving.

I was recently discussing this with a friend, who said, "I understand your premise that politics are going to affect behavior, but how can you predict what that effect is going to be? Couldn't you just as easily conclude that the economy is good now, people are unhappy with the insanity around them, so they are going to divert themselves by buying things and running away on vacation?" That's a good question. You can't necessarily predict how people are going to react to a particular change. You have to watch and test and measure to see how they respond. But the important thing is that you need to be aware that a change, some change, is going to happen and be prepared to come up with your own response.

What's Aspirin Got to Do with Detergent?

Trends and events in one market can also provide valuable insights to people in seemingly unrelated markets. A new brand

"When you see the fabulous success of Four Seasons, you have to ask yourself: What's the message for me in my market?"

or the new positioning of a brand changes the molecular structure of a category, but it also changes the molecular structure of other categories. Look at what happened with analgesics. We started with plain, old aspirin. Then Tylenol came along and said it would relieve pain better and wouldn't upset your stomach. This upped the ante on pain relief, which led to extra strength this and extra strength that, and the entry of Motrin and Advil. It also added the stomach-irritation factor, which resulted in coated aspirin. Next came the ease with which any of these can be swallowed, which led to the introduction of Caplets and pills. As the new attributes entered the dialogue, pain relief lost center stage. Finally, along came Aleve, which brought things full circle by promising better pain relief.

What can other marketers learn from this? Well, one thing you can learn is that even when consumers are apparently happy with a product, it's not all that hard to change the dialogue and make then unhappy. Detergent marketers certainly know this, because basically the same thing happened in detergents as with analgesics. First, the dialogue in the detergent market was about which product cleans best. Then they introduced extra concentrate, which combined cleaning better with being easy to carry. Then came easy-to-use liquids, and now they are back to which product cleans best.

What's going on in your market? How can you change the

dialogue? Is there potential for an alternative product that does or doesn't do *x, y,* and *z* that your product doesn't or does do now?

Think about hotels. Why do some hotel chains like the Four Seasons have such success? Who said that we needed those terry cloth robes and all that shampoo and soap? Heck that stuff is expensive! Other hotels are cutting those things to improve profitability. What does Four Seasons know that the others don't? Maybe the other guys are too concerned about cost efficiencies and personnel controls while Four Seasons runs away with the profits and a satisfied consumer base that will come again and again. But when you see the fabulous success of Four Seasons, you have to ask yourself: What's the message for me in my market?

The entrepreneurs who started double drive-through restaurants like Rally's looked at the long lines at McDonald's drive-through windows and saw that they could skim off customers and reduce their real-estate and facilities needs by offering a stripped-down menu and offering only drive-through service. It worked great until they made the mistake of expanding the menu and creating the same long lines as at McDonald's. Are the Hertz platinum cards that get your car brought to you at the curb like in the old days a reaction to a dissatisfaction with the way that airports operate?

You have to look at what other marketers are doing and analyze why they are doing it. At Coke, we always went to food shows, not so much to show what we had but to see what other people were doing. We looked at the packaging and the trends in color or wrappings. But we didn't go just to food shows. We also went to auto shows and to cosmetic shows and fashion shows, because those industries are in the lead on form and color, and to sports shows to find out about sizes and levels of aggressiveness on the part of consumers.

Like politicians, all of these people are marketers. They are all putting something in front of consumers for them to vote on, to choose, to drive, to photograph, to use, or to eat. Anything that they know, you need to learn. If you do, you will succeed more than your competition.

Get Them While You Have Them

There's another important way of focusing on consumers that I don't think marketers pay enough attention to, and that's on building relationships with them.

"Instead of trying to wring the last dollar out of me today, the people in the eyeglass store should be working to make sure that I'm coming back."

I have said before that I absolutely don't believe in the premise, "Get them young and they'll be yours forever." Yeah, get them young, but then you have to market to them forever. But that doesn't mean that you should view every sale as a one-time event. In fact, the easiest people in the world to market to, and the best customers who buy the most stuff at the highest prices, are the people who have already used your product or service and are pleased with it. So it astounds me when I go into a store or buy a product and nobody says or does anything to get me to come back. Or worse yet, I get shabby treatment. The marketer has already invested the money to get me interested in the first place, and now I'm pissed off. What a waste!

Repeat sales are very effective, and very few companies actually work on getting them. Frequent-flyer and frequent-buyer programs are one way to go after repeat sales, but they can be very expensive, and they only work in businesses where the customers have a fairly steady continuing need for the product. There are lots of other, simpler things that companies could do to woo repeat customers, without spending a lot.

Eyeglass stores are a great example of places where the salespeople are so focused on selling you expensive options today that they miss the chance to get you to come back. I am always breaking, losing, or deciding I don't like my glasses, so I am a good customer for eyeglass stores. Or at least I could be. But every time I go into one, I get the hard sell about picking more expensive frames and photosensitive, lightweight lenses and getting coatings and ultraviolet protection and all kinds of other stuff. When I walk out, the clerks are doing high fives because they've sold me all of this big-ticket stuff, but I'm feeling like I've been had. What they don't seem to think about is that I am going to buy another pair of glasses in just a few months and more pairs after that. And when I do, am I going to go back there? No. They have done nothing to build a relationship with me.

Instead of trying to wring the last dollar out of me today, the people in the eyeglass store should be working to make sure that I'm coming back. The fact that I've come to the store means that you probably have already got my sale today, so what you need to concentrate on is the next sale. You have to be figuring out how to sell the second pair before the consumer walks out of your store. How hard would it have been to have the clerk make a note to call me the next day and ask me if I liked the glasses? If you do this, you will be able to fix whatever was wrong, maybe establish a relationship with that customer and make sure that he or she comes to see you again. When I take my car to the dealership, they call me after the service to ask me how my car is. I think this is so smart because it means that if I have a problem, I don't stew over it for months and months.

Goodwill Counts

I moved to Atlanta twenty years ago. Every Christmas since then, I have gotten a letter from the CEO of the Southern

"If [a marketer] has done a really good job, its customers will even be suspicious of anyone else who comes along."

Company, which is the company that I buy my electricity from. At the beginning, I found the whole concept to be a little absurd. Here was a guy who was actually selling me a product that I couldn't get anywhere else, and he was sending me a letter thanking me for buying my electricity from him. So it intrigued me, and that is all I needed for me to want to investigate further.

I found the whole process, as I started to study and learn over time, absolutely fantastic. This guy understood unequivocally that sooner or later he was going to need me to be in his court. I did not know in what form, and I'm not even sure he did, but he was smart enough to establish the relationship early.

It turns out, Atlanta is a very green town. There are trees all over town, which makes Atlanta a fabulous place to live. Atlanta also is an old town, which means that most of the electricity infrastructure was put in many years ago. This means that in Atlanta, we have electricity poles and we have cables going from pole to pole. As Atlanta is also in the South, we get a lot of storms, and when you get a storm, trees tend to be blown over. What this means is that trees fall on poles, cable breaks, electricity goes out. And the customers get upset.

It can take a lot of time for the electricity to be restored. As a matter of fact, four years ago we were without electricity for about ten days. Boy, did I remember that Christmas letter from Bill Dalberg precisely at that time. The reservoir of goodwill that Bill had directly built with me is what actually made him whole when we were without electricity. My attitude was real simple. I know they're out there trying to fix the electricity as fast as they can.

For reasons like this alone, building relationships in marketing is really important. If you build enough of a reservoir of goodwill for your brands, when you have problems, your customers are going to be a lot more forgiving.

There is another, and perhaps more important, reason for building customer relationships. That's because, if you have a relationship with your customers, they are more likely to stick with you when your product comes under attack by another brand. As a matter of fact the electricity saga continues, because now electricity is being deregulated like the telephones. So the question for power companies is going to be, whether they have built enough of a reservoir of goodwill in order for consumers to be loyal to them. If they have done a really good job, their customers will actually be suspicious of anyone else who comes along. Most customers don't know anything about electricity except that they need it and they need it all the time. So if power companies have been really conscientious and reliable and built enough goodwill, when another guy comes along with a cheaper price, not only are the customers not going to be interested, but they are also going to be downright doubtful about the other guy's product.

What more could you ask for? Look at how many people still have AT&T long-distance service. I get the phone calls every day asking me to switch, but AT&T has done a good job of convincing me that it will continue to take care of me, and I reward them with my business.

You can translate this lesson to just about every product and service in the market. Sooner or later, you're going to go through cycles in which the consumer is going to be faced with an economic uncertainty or a product that has been presented in a different way and that fundamentally says, "Listen, I can give you everything that the other guy is doing or giving you, except cheaper, smaller, bigger, or faster." If you have the mindset that you need to build that reservoir of goodwill over the years, you'll have that reservoir to draw on when you need it. And believe me, the day will come when you will need it.

It may cost a few extra pennies today to build bridges and make friends with customers. But if you pay attention to them, if you think about their needs and wants and feelings, if you take the time and make the effort to think broadly and learn everything you can about them, it will pay off immeasurably. If you don't, you can hang up your hat and close your doors because somebody else will—and you will be out of business.

6

WHAT JERRY SEINFELD CAN TEACH YOU ABOUT MARKETING

I recently talked to a client who was jumping up and down, nearly wetting his pants in excitement because a new survey showed that his product had the top brand awareness in the category. He had saturated the territory with a big ad campaign, and now the research indicated that millions of consumers thought of his brand first when they thought about products in that category.

"That's great," I said when he told me. "And what about sales? How are you converting them?" I asked.

"Oh," he said, "well, the ads were so successful that we are just going to keep using them for a while."

There you have a textbook example of how to waste money in marketing. And yet in my experience, it is a mistake that marketing people make *all the time*. The problem is that my client had done only half the job. Yet he thought he was finished. He had spent a ton of money to create an image for his product, and now he was just going to sit back and hope that it would sell.

What was missing?

He hadn't asked the consumer to actually buy his product.

Go Ahead: Ask Them to Buy Your Product

One of the things that has always baffled me is the notion among marketers that asking people to buy your product is just too crass for words. "Oh no," they declare. "Asking is too direct, it's not something we would want to do. Marketing is supposed to create an image, an aura that appeals to people. Don't go too far and offend consumers by asking for the order."

Well, I don't get that.

"Jerry Seinfeld once described to me the metrics of a joke. 'It has to have,' he explained, 'a setup, a delivery, and a punch line!' Marketing does too."

I'll be as quick as anyone to tell you that image is important. Consumers have to have a clear idea in their minds about what a product stands for—quality, speed, low price, high price, variety, whatever it is—before they will even consider actually buying it. But creating an image is only the first step. Your goal is to get people to pull out their wallets and pay for your product. And the best way I know to do that is to give them reasons to buy it— it tastes good, it will get you there faster, it's reliable, you'll smell better. And then you need to actually ask them to buy it.

I am on the record as being the person who pulled the plug on rerunning Coke's famous Hilltop campaign. That was the one where we set up a bunch of kids from all over the world on the top of a hill and had them chirp "I'd like to teach the world to sing."

I know, you loved that ad. Everyone loved that ad.

Like the Mean Joe Greene ad, it was a wildly popular commercial with consumers and bottlers. And I didn't stop using it because I didn't like it—I actually loved the film. It's touching, warm, and a great vehicle to promote unity among the different people of the world. As a matter of fact, in 1979 when the ad was first introduced, I was working on the Coke account for McCann-Erickson in Mexico. We adapted the ad; we even found a Mexican girl who had been on the shoot and featured her in a bunch of ancillary marketing activities.

But did that ad sell any more Coke?

Nope.

All it did was give people a nice, warm, fuzzy feeling about Coca-Cola. In fact, it was so unsuccessful that we lost market share the entire time it ran, especially in the United States.

On the other hand, think about the car salesmen. Yes, I said car salesmen. Or turn on the television late at night and watch one of those infomercials where the personalities are peddling all kinds of gadgets and other things that we really don't need. They come on at you with the straightforward old salesmen's pitch, talking about features and benefits. They explain in unequivocal terms why the new abdominizer, juicer, or blender is actually going to make our lives better. Then they ask us to pick up the phone and shell out twenty dollars or two hundred, *and we do.*

Why don't we use this approach in marketing on an ongoing basis? Marketing is not the same thing as sales or advertising, but it has to include both. Jerry Seinfeld once described to me the metrics of a joke. "It has to have a setup, a delivery, and a punch line!" Marketing does too. It must have a setup: the reason for the product; a delivery: the reason to buy; and the punch line—buy it please!

Awareness Is Just the First Step

When you think about it, advertising awareness and brand awareness are pretty easy things to create. I can generate advertising awareness with no problem. All I need to do is get on television and take my shirt off, and people will remember the advertising. I can generate brand awareness by naming my brand Kaboom or something like that, and people will remember my

**"You don't want virtual consumption. . . .
You don't want people who love you
but never buy you."**

brand. I can actually even generate favorite brand status by creating an image of luxury like the Ferrari and Lamborghini folks, or by running really charming and endearing ads like Kodak. But even being the favorite brand doesn't get you to where you need to be, because being consumers' favorite doesn't necessarily mean that you are going to make the sale.

I learned a lot about the favorite-brand trap when I was at Coca-Cola. In the early 1980s, survey after survey showed that Coca-Cola was the winner when you asked people what was their favorite soft-drink brand. But at the same time, while our status as favorite brand was going up, our brand consumption was decreasing. We were losing share even though people loved our brand, loved our advertising, and loved what we stood for.

That's when we realized that we were dealing with a phenomenon that I call virtual consumption.

Virtual consumption is what a lot of luxury goods like sports cars have. Everybody says, "Wow. Swell. They're great. I love them. They are my favorite brand." But when you ask when or if they are going to buy one, they say "Oh no. I can't afford one" or "It doesn't suit my needs or my lifestyle" or "I like it, but I can get a better deal on something else" or "It doesn't come in the color I want." What you have here are people who think they are in love with you, but who have no plans to marry you. In some cases, they'll even buy the T-shirt and wear your advertising, and because of that they will *think* that they are using your product when they aren't. This is all very flattering, but it doesn't spell success.

You don't want virtual consumption. You don't want people who love you but never buy you, just as you don't want people who are aware of who you are, how you look, or what you do but have no interest in you. You shouldn't have any interest in them either. What you need is sales.

In chapter 4 I talked about branding, positioning, and creating images that differentiate your product or service from the competition. It is definitely important to control the dialogue in the market and to make sure that consumers see your product as different, better, and special. But that is only the tee up. You still have to swing the club and drive the ball by convincing consumers that not only is your product different, better, and special—but that it is also something that they want to buy. And then you have to get them to actually go out and buy it. Closing the sale is part of the job of marketing.

The way I look at it is that there are three levels of interest that consumers can show in your product. The first is brand awareness. They know who you are. The second is what is generally called purchase intent. This is when a potential customer says that he or she knows of your product and intends to buy it someday. But as good as this sounds, this term is misleading, and marketers who are satisfied with having "high levels of purchase intent" are going to be sadly disappointed when those good intentions aren't realized. Then there is a third level, which is the one you should really care about. It is share of future purchases: Are they planning to buy it? Out of your next three, five, or ten purchases, how many of them are going to be my product? After you create awareness, this is the measure you need to work on.

Consumption Is What Counts

Many traditional marketers and most ad agencies would argue that my client who had successfully nabbed the top spot in his category had not made a mistake. They would say that the guy had in fact done his job because he created awareness. Selling is what salespeople do, they might add—it's not marketing. But

"The old conventional thinking that said if you grab people's hearts, their wallets will follow is dead, kaput, finished. . . . people need reasons to buy."

let's not forget that the only reason to have marketing is to sell more stuff, so if marketers aren't increasing consumption, they *aren't* doing their job. Awareness is important, but sales and profit are everything.

The old conventional thinking that said if you grab people's hearts, their wallets will follow is dead, kaput, finished. Just think about a political race. Do you vote for the candidate you think is a nice guy? Or do you vote for the one who takes a stand on the issues and tells you what he or she is going to do for you and your favorite causes?

It's the same with products. If your goal is to sell more stuff, you need to give people reasons to buy. Simply knowing about your product isn't enough. So beyond just creating awareness, you've got to do whatever it takes to get your message through to them. And if you want them to keep coming back for more and with increasing frequency, you have to give them more reasons. Essentially, you need to say, "Look, you need my stuff. Or, if you don't need my stuff, you think you need my stuff. Or, at least, you want my stuff. Here's why. So go buy it." Again and again.

Dimensionalize: More Reasons to Buy Equal More Sales

Great concept, you're saying. Of course you want people to buy your product. But how do you get people to do that? And how is your way of transforming theoretical interest into actual sales any different from traditional marketing?

You do it by dimensionalizing. Dimensionalizing means giving people more and more reasons to buy beyond the apparent

---

"Coke was an old and well-known product, but all of a sudden sales took off . . . because we gave more customers in more segments of the market more reasons to buy it."

---

or the original selling proposition, that is, you add dimensions to the image of the product in consumers' minds. And the way that I do it differently, and I think that all marketers are going to have to do it, is by looking at consumers in new and creative ways in order to come up with new and different dimensions.

Traditionally marketers have thought about targeting, and therefore dimensionalizing, in terms of only three or four broad demographic categories: age, gender, ethnicity, and maybe income or professional versus nonprofessional status. And once they have come up with three or four dimensions, or appeals or reasons that each of these groups should buy, they have played them over and over again.

Well, my point of view is that that isn't enough. Yes, it's true that you often appeal to older people in different ways from younger people and men differently from women. But if you stop and think about it, there are a lot more categories or segments of the market and a lot more dimensions that you can add. And you need to add dimensions not only to appeal to new categories of customers, but also to keep the old ones coming back.

At Coca-Cola, when we seriously started dimensionalizing in the early 1990s with the launch of the "Always Coca-Cola" campaign, we came up with thirty-five different attributes or dimensions that we used to convince customers to buy Coke. And yes, the Always campaign actually provided thirty-five different ways to see the brand, and we created thirty-five different TV commercials at one time, something that was previously unheard of. Whenever you turned on your television, we were telling you that Coke was not only refreshing, but sociable, trendy, reliable, smart, cool, and all sorts of other things. And it worked. Coke was an old and well-known product, but all of a sudden sales took off. This was the period when Coca-Cola Comany's sales jumped fifty percent, to fifteen billion cases a year, in just five years, all because we gave more customers in more segments of the market more reasons to buy it.

One way of segmenting the market that I have found very helpful is to look at consumption patterns and then look at the image or brand dimensions among these different groups. What you will find surprising are the radical differences among the light, medium, and heavy users regarding the specifics that you will think are foundational attributes of your product. Further, there are big differences not only between the people who consume lots of your product and people who only buy it occasionally; there are vast differences between people who frequently buy your product and those who regularly support your competitors.

This information is valuable for two very important reasons. One is that heavy users are obviously more profitable for you than light users. So once you recognize them as a specific segment, you can then tailor your marketing to maintain and increase the usage of your heavy consumers and to win your competitors' heavy consumers. The other is that when you figure out what it is that is appealing to heavy users of your product, you can use that information to help convert some of the light users.

What we found at Coke was that heavy users generally could give us a lot more reasons for buying the product than light users. So what we learned was that we needed to figure out how to get the light users to relate to more reasons the same way the heavy users did.

Think about it. If I drink a Coke for refreshment and nothing else, I will drink Coke. However if I drink Coke for ten reasons, it follows that I will drink much more.

Using heavy users as a model for targeting light users is a good idea for marketing discretionary products like soft drinks, where drinking or not drinking is simply a matter of preference. As much as I hate to admit it, soft drinks are not essential. So it's possible to convince the light users to care about some of the same attributes as the heavy users. In other businesses, such as airlines, however, the heavy users may be fundamentally different from the light users. Heavy users fly a lot because they have to. Light users generally fly only when the price makes it appealing or when they are going on vacation or to a wedding or other family function. What this means is that in these businesses, you have to appeal to the two different segments in radically different ways.

Unfortunately, I'm not sure that most airlines truly understand this. Otherwise, why would they rely so heavily on frequent-flyer programs? Think about it. In a frequent-flyer program, you are rewarding with more travel those people who already travel all the time. I travel two million miles a year, and then the airlines give me the opportunity to travel another 300,000 for free. I, quite frankly, don't want to take another flight if I don't need to.

The hotel guys get this. They went from giving you points at Holiday Inn, Sheraton, or Ramada, to throwing a *USA Today* in front of your door and putting you on the floor that was baptized as the Executive Floor (which actually was no different from the floor you stayed on last time). Still, you get the impression that they care about your business when they recognize you as special and different from others who only occasionally patronize their hotels. These people understand the profitability of the heavy user.

In the soft-drink business, we knew, after a long time and lots of analysis, that we wanted to own the daily drinkers. In countries like Mexico, where per capita's are four hundred six-ounce servings per year, the daily drinkers are those who probably drink three or four soft drinks per day, or even more. These are the consumers you want, and you want to make sure that you capture all of them.

If you have a thirty percent share of a market overall, you want to make sure that you have at least twice as many of the daily drinkers. If the daily drinkers account for ten percent of the total category business, you need to take as many of them as you can. Let the competition have the monthly or occasional users. Develop programs that address heavy users. This will trickle down to the other users, but your business will be much more profitable and you will be significantly happier if you do this.

Think Like a Politician

Another way to segment the market is to do what the politicians do and look at loyalty or how strongly a consumer favors or

> **"(If) you have lots of people in the soft support and undecided categories . . . start putting your product in megapackages."**

doesn't favor your product. By and large, political constituencies break into the following categories: hard support, soft support, undecided, soft opposition, and hard opposition. The hard support will vote for you in the middle of a blizzard. They'll vote regardless of what you say or do. The soft support needs a little bit of convincing, but not a lot, they are the ones who are in your court. The undecided are the fence-sitters, the ones who will make the decision the day before the election on the basis of what you told them in the last couple of days or what you told them about your opponent. The soft opposition will consider you but are hard to move, and you may as well just forget about the hard opposition—they'll never vote for you.

Once you recognize these differences, you can start thinking about distinct offers that are going to appeal to each segment. For example, one thing you can do in markets where you have lots of people in the soft support and undecided categories is to start putting your product in megapackages. Eight-packs of paper towels, twenty-four-can cases of Coca-Cola, six-packs of tissues. What this means is that you only have to make one sale, and you can keep the consumer out of the market for a while, so it will be a long time before he or she makes another purchase, which might go to your competitor.

This strategy, however, is never going to work with people who oppose you. But you generally shouldn't bother with them because to sell to them you're probably going to have to spend a lot of money for not much return. The soft opposition is get-table, but big packages are just going to turn them off. No matter how economical you make them, people who think that they don't like your product are not going to go out and buy a ton of it. For the soft opposition, you need to do more things like trial-size giveaways and incentives to make a second purchase. And for all categories, you have to keep trying out new dimensions and giving people more reasons to try to decide that they prefer your brand.

The tactics that you choose are, of course, going to have to depend on a lot of other variables in addition to support or opposition levels. You have to look further to figure out why people are supporting or not supporting you. In Venezuela, for example, for decades Pepsi was the dominant player. It had eighty percent of the market. But that support was very soft because it was based mainly on distribution. Pepsi was more readily available than Coke, so people knew it better and decided it was okay. But when Coke basically bought out the Pepsi bottler in Venezuela and started a baseball-based campaign to win the hearts and wallets of the Venezuelan public, it quickly won more than ninety percent of the market.

Sometimes people oppose you because they think they don't like something about you, and sometimes because they just like your competition better. Most often, people are undecided because they just don't know enough about any of the products in the market. I sometimes call the undecideds the uneducated, because they just need a lot more information. As a marketer, if you give them enough information, and the right information, they will decide, and they will decide to buy your product.

There is no single strategy or group of strategies that is going to work with everyone in a specific category. And most of the strategies that you use will work to some degree in more than one category. So knowing where someone falls on the loyalty spectrum is not going to give you an instant, surefire sales pitch. You still have to test and measure and keep giving people new reasons to buy and use your product. But if you look at people in terms of their loyalty at the same time that you look at their usage levels, age, gender, and ethnicity, you will do a much better job creating the most effective programs.

Never Stop Adding Reasons

You must constantly expand the definition of why people should buy your product, both intrinsically and extrinsically. This is what I mean when I talk about Generation W-H-Y. What

---

"Like all marketers who claim that they are in mature businesses, we were just being lazy."

---

most marketers today don't realize is that it's not enough to focus on the Boomers, the Xers, the Tweeners, or Generation Y. The common characteristic that cuts across all demographics is W-H-Y: Why the hell should I buy your product?

You don't want to stop telling consumers that aspirin will cure their headaches. But what else can you tell them? Can you tell them that you have a better package? Or a coating that won't irritate their stomachs? Keep renewing the proposition in order to keep giving people reasons to buy your product or service and not the competition's.

A while ago I read someplace a quote that pointed out that even if you don't want to change the color of your house, if it's white and you want it to stay white, you still have to repaint it periodically. If you don't, you're going to have a gray house. A brand is the same. If you want your brand to be fresh, you have to refresh its meaning and definition over and over again. If not, consumers will take it for granted. Your brand will fade with time and your volume will begin to decrease.

Charles Schwab has done a great job of refreshing its brand. Its primary consumer offering is low-cost brokerage services. It's been that since the day it opened, and it hasn't changed. But look at their ads. They constantly remind you of who they are and what they do, and then they add something else. We're a low-cost broker, and we can give you research information. We're a low-cost broker, and we're on the Internet. In this case, you could argue that Schwab isn't even really adding dimensions, in the sense that they are just enumerating one more quality that is inherent to what they do. But in any event, what they are doing is listing more and more reasons for people to like them. And given their success on-line, it seems to be working.

In the old days at Coke, we thought that because people already knew Coke, there was nothing else we could tell them. We thought we were a mature business without a lot of growth potential left. How wrong we were! Like all marketers who claim that they are in mature businesses, we were just being lazy. There are always more things you can tell people and ways that you can help them identify and relate to your product. At the time, Coke had only four or five definitions or dimensions that we continually pitched. It was refreshing, thirst quenching, bubbly, delicious, and social. So we began thinking about what else we could tell people. And we came up with the thirty-five dimensions that were associated with "Always": Coke is part of my life. It understands me. Cool people drink it. People of all ages drink it. It has a bite and a distinctive taste. It comes in a contour bottle. It is modern, funny, emotional, simple, large, friendly, consistent, and everywhere.

This was the time when we started using the associative imagery of sports. But we didn't use sports just to sponsor things so that we could put our logo up in big stadiums. We used sports affiliations as a way to bond with consumers by being relevant and involved in what they care about. It's like that ancient Chinese proverb: tell them and they will forget. Show them and they will remember. Involve them and they will understand. We involved consumers in what they wanted (the passion of sports) AND we asked them to buy more of our product. Our slogan for the soccer World Cup was: eat football, sleep football, and drink Coca-Cola.

Get it? The consumer certainly did.

We also started running commercials and promotions suggesting specific times when a Coke would be just right. Isn't having a Coke a festive way to celebrate New Year's and Christmas? Isn't it great refreshment to break your Ramadan fast? Can you imagine a picnic without Coca-Cola? Oh, and by the way, kids, you can also get discounts at all kinds of different places if you buy Coke.

In the past, Coke had certainly used a variety of advertising, but there weren't all that many dimensions, and they weren't consciously designed to appeal to specific segments of the market. They weren't part of a coherent strategy. Of course, even though Coke means many things to people today, things won't stay that way. Loyalty and attachment are perishable. The company will have to continue to broaden that definition, and if it doesn't, the definition will narrow by itself.

This constant redefining and refreshing of your product is very hard work. You have to get up every morning thinking of yet another reason why people might want to buy your stuff. And you will run into a lot of resistance. Your advertising agencies won't want to do the work of coming up with a new campaign. So they will try to tell you that you may need another commercial, but you don't need another definition. The packaging guys will fall in love with their package that just won them an award and they won't want to change it. And even management will start to get nervous about your relentless drive not to leave well enough alone.

But don't give up. Do it and do it and do it. This is the way of the future. If this doesn't happen, the status quo will erode, and when your brand erodes, your volume will too.

Expand the Market by Redefining It

One big lesson that everybody should learn from Starbucks is that, even though consumers have to understand your product if you want them to buy it, sometimes consumers can understand a product too well. By that I mean, sometimes people will fix a product in their minds as being for Purpose A, and then you have

"Anytime someone starts understanding your product or service, it's time to reinvent it."

to work real hard to get them to see that it can also serve Purpose B and C. But the rewards can be enormous. In Starbucks' case, everybody thought that they understood coffee quite well until Starbucks came along and reexplained things. No, Starbucks said, coffee is not just caffeine delivered in the form of some ground-up beans and water. And, no, you don't just want it to wake up in the morning and after a meal. Instead, Starbucks told us, coffee drinking is an experience, and you should drink it any time that you want to be social, want some variety in your life, need a break or a treat. If you understand this and you know about coffee, you will be a smart and savvy person.

Once Starbucks explained it this way, not only did it win customers from its competitors, but it also got a lot more people to start drinking a lot more coffee. It actually expanded the market.

GE Capital did the same thing several years ago when it decided to change its focus from expanding its share of the existing truck leasing market to getting more companies to lease instead of buy their trucks. In the past, the primary reason that a company would decide to lease was that it didn't want to invest the money to buy a fleet of trucks. But then GE came along and said, look, if you lease from us, we will manage your fleet and do all the servicing and scheduling and you won't have to do anything, except pay us. By expanding the reasons for leasing it attracted a bunch of new customers into the market.

Computer companies have done the same thing. The market for word processing is pretty limited, but by redefining computers as being not just office equipment but also communications vehicles, entertainment centers, educational tools, and shopping resources, computer companies have expanded the market at phenomenal rates.

Remember that anytime someone starts understanding your

product or service, it's time to reinvent it. The ski industry is going through some tough times of late, and I think that it's because consumers think they already have such a clear idea in their minds about what skiing is. Just think about it. Skiing has always been associated with being cold. It's often a hassle to get there because of the snow. People have accidents, sometimes serious, all the time. And it's expensive. Yes, it's also exhilarating and fun and a great escape from the rest of your life. But often, only one person in a family really likes to ski, so everyone else is bored and complaining. This is definitely a drawback.

What the ski industry needs to do is to expand the definition of the ski trip to include other benefits that will appeal to more people. Some of those benefits are already there, but they need to be emphasized and explained better. What if people thought a ski trip meant fine dining, pampering at the spa, and great shopping? I bet that a lot more people would be interested.

In order to sell stuff, you have to continually come up with new reasons why a person *might* want to buy something, experience something, learn something, eat something. Then you have to systematically test these ideas in order to discover which do the best job of actually moving people to pull out their wallets and purchase.

The general concept of dimensionalizing that I've been talking about here isn't new, but like many of the other things I talk about in this book, the extent and the persistence with which I think it has to be done is. Always keep your eye on the consumers. To understand them, you have to consciously and constantly work at coming up with new ways to get them to buy. Don't ever forget that your goal isn't to entertain or intrigue them. It's to sell them your product or service.

Pay Attention to Conversion Rates

One way to keep focused on finding things that really sell stuff is to make conversion rates one of the key measurements that you track. Retailers do this by counting how many of the people

**"You know that they are already interested
or they wouldn't be (in the store).
What do you need to do to make the sale?"**

who come into the store actually buy something. The fast-food business measures incidence, or the number of high-profit side items such as fries and drinks, that it sells along with the low-profit burgers and chicken. You figure that it cost a lot of money to run advertising and promotions to get people into your store, so how well are you doing in selling them stuff once they come in? You know that they are already interested or they wouldn't be there. What do you need to do to make the sale?

Obviously, the more potential consumers you convert into actual buyers, the more efficient your initial marketing spending becomes.

There are a lot of ways to increase conversion rates. If your product is sold in stores, on-site promotions are obviously one of them. Another is to make it easy for customers to make a purchase. This means having enough people available and having them properly trained to help people find what they want. And, of course, you need enough cashiers to take their money when they want to give it to you. If you are in the catalog business, it means having enough people to answer the telephones and providing prompt shipping and easy returns. I would also suggest that catalog companies, which need to get the people who receive their catalogs to actually open them up and read them, could raise their sales simply by following up with a postcard or a phone call that says, "Hey did you get our catalog? And, by the way, if you buy something in the next five days, we'll give you a discount or a special gift."

Yesterday, I called up the Road Runners Club to order a running mask, and a very nice woman on the phone sold me a ton of other stuff simply by looking at my past orders and figuring out what I was interested in or might need.

I know that most purchases today aren't made over the telephone or in situations where a salesperson has access to my individual buying history. But this will happen more and more in the future, as more purchases are made on-line and customer data is tracked and stored accordingly. Even if you don't have access to that kind of information right now, it's the direction you need to be thinking about. In the future, the way to sell products more efficiently and successfully is to focus on smaller and smaller segments and then tailor your offering to meet their needs.

Think of Dell, which only builds the components you want into your PC with only the specifications you require.

And finally, there's the obvious way to sell stuff. One of the very best ways to get people to buy your stuff is to simply *ask* them. You can spend hundreds of millions of dollars on creating brands and images and giving people possible reasons to buy, but you're leaving consumers open to your competitors if you don't come out and say "Go buy my stuff."

Indeed, this is perhaps the one marketing technique that many of the old-style, highbrow artsy marketers will refuse to accept. Perhaps it's because they don't want to admit that their job is to sell stuff, and they don't want to be held accountable in case it doesn't sell. But, like it or not, awards and high-toned commercials aren't what counts. Sales do. If you ask consumers to buy your products, they will—perhaps not always, but at least more often than if you don't. And that's more sales for you, and fewer for your competitors.

7

FISH WHERE
THE FISH ARE

In the early 1990s, The Coca-Cola Company, like many others, rushed into Russia, Eastern Europe, and Central Asia to cash in on the newly opened markets for western products. We built plants, bought trucks, set up distribution lines. Wow, were we excited. Hundreds of millions of thirsty consumers would now have Coke products available to them.

And boy, did we miss a big opportunity.

We weren't the only ones. Foreign companies by the score have been writing down assets and pulling back in the former Communist Bloc. We had all fallen for the *Field of Dreams* theory of marketing: if you build the distribution system and make a product available, people will buy it.

They didn't.

In retrospect, I could argue that the headlong rush into these countries was simply another case of scientific calculation and experimentation. A potential opportunity existed, so we needed to take a shot at it. And I could point out that in the general environment of excitement, it didn't seem as if we could afford to let the competition get a jump on us. If they had succeeded, no matter how successfully we were investing our money elsewhere, we would have been seen as slow-footed losers. But we made a big mistake, not because we took a risk and tried to expand globally, but because we didn't do our homework, we didn't understand the markets well enough, and, therefore, we didn't market as aggressively as we should have.

Where's the Money?

The thing that we should have remembered is that expansion, whether it's into new markets or new products, should never

---

"You would never buy a stock just to build a portfolio without considering whether the investment was likely to be profitable."

---

be undertaken just because the market is there or you can make the product. Just as you would never buy a stock just to build a portfolio without considering whether the investment was likely to be profitable, you should never go into a new market or introduce a new product without seriously stopping to consider how you are going create a profitable new business.

The first thing that you have to consider when you are thinking about entering a new market is whether there is willingness or need on the part of the consumers to buy your product. In other words, the question isn't how many people are in a particular market but how many people there are who might want your product *and* have the money to buy it.

Many years ago Coca-Cola was forced to get out of India because the Indian government asked the company for its formula and the company refused to give it to them. Eventually, through the hard work of many people, we were able to go back into India, and we rubbed our hands in glee at the potential of over a billion people buying our products in India. But then we realized that most of those billion people don't have any money to buy soft drinks or much of anything else. Until more Indians have more disposable income, there isn't going to be much of a market in India for much of anything. The same was true in many parts of the former Communist Bloc. We weren't prudent. We didn't quantify the true potential and invest accordingly.

The Biggest Potential May Be at Home

Over the years, entering new markets through distributive expansion has been an obvious and easy fallback for many

---

**"Existing markets tend to produce better results than new markets. That's in part because you already have brand awareness, even among people who aren't consumers.
You don't have to spend the money to introduce and establish yourself all over again."**

---

companies seeking growth. However, if your goal is to maximize your return on investment, this often isn't the smartest way to go. What you need to do is to concentrate first on the markets that have the most potential—which are usually the markets that you are already in—and make sure that you are maximizing all of them. Only then should you think about trekking into other markets. You must never forget that to sell your products, you need willing consumers with money to spend. This is what I mean when I say: fish where the fish are.

When we at Coca-Cola were debating about whether we could continue to grow the business by going into new countries, Roberto Goizueta came up with a great line.

"Look," he said, "every person in the world drinks about sixty-four ounces of liquid a day. Coca-Cola products account for only about two of those ounces today." Previously, we had been looking at the potential market as two ounces multiplied by 5.6 billion people in the world. What Roberto was saying was that the more fruitful course would be not to think only of getting more people to drink our products, but also to think of getting the people who were already drinking our products to drink *more* of them, at the expense of other liquids. The implication was that there was still a huge market to be developed out there among the billions of customers that we already had.

My perspective has always been that existing markets tend to produce better results than new markets. That's in part because you already have brand awareness, even among people who aren't consumers. You don't have to spend the money to introduce and establish yourself all over again. But perhaps more importantly, it's because you have a better chance of selling stuff to people who already want it.

Your hit rate with people who are already either frequent or infrequent customers is a lot greater than with people who aren't really interested in your product or have never even considered buying it. Think about it. If you are marketing sanitary napkins, are you going to sell more in a market of a hundred women or a market of a thousand men? The facts may be a little different here because men don't have much physical use for sanitary napkins, but the concept and the math are the same. You have a better chance of selling your product to people who think that they need or want it than to people who don't. Your success rate is going to be a lot higher.

I recently spoke at a ski industry event. The ski people were focusing on a strategy to convince nonskiers to ski. This made no sense at all to me. I advised them to change their strategy because it would be a hell of a lot easier to convince those who already ski to ski more first than it would be to try to convince new folks of the value and allure of skiing.

It's easy to lose sight of this and to get blinded by visible demand. For established products like Coke, for example, entering new markets is an easy way to get short-term growth because there is generally some level of spillover demand from your visibility in other markets. But to really build sustainable demand, entering new markets is very inefficient. You can spend a lot less and sell a lot more in existing markets where the consumer knows about your products and service. You do have to get them to increment and broaden their behavior. You have to convince them to buy more or to use your product to replace something else that they are buying. But that's a much more productive activity than trying to convert people who just aren't interested.

I don't mean to suggest in any way that incrementing and broadening the behavior of current consumers is easy. It isn't. In fact, the more your brand is developed in a market, the harder it is going to be to get that incremental sale. You will have to broaden the definition of what your brand or product is, and you will have to spend money to make sure you reach the people in the market who aren't currently buying. And you have to reach the people who are buying more often to give them more reasons to buy. Still, with your brand awareness already developed, you have a better chance of getting greater success than in an entirely new market.

Create P&Ls by Brand, by Market

So how much money do you spend? When do you decide that the old market is saturated and that investing in new markets is, in fact, the better course? As I have said many times before, it all boils

> **"Most of the time, I'll bet my money on existing markets."**

down to figuring out whether you can make money, how much, and by when. In other words, you must figure out what your profit and loss statement is for each brand for a specific period.

My point of view is that you need to spend as much money as you can until the return investment is no longer acceptable.

So you need to evaluate whether you should enter a market on the basis of the return on investment. You have to figure out the returns in the new market, then compare them with your existing markets. Most of the time, I'll bet my money on existing markets.

The same thing is true for brands as is true for countries. You have to assemble the numbers and use them. Unfortunately, very few marketers do this. Lots of companies are great at collecting sales figures by the day or by the hour; they'd do it by the minute if they could. But they only attach them to costs every three months, or longer. As a result they really don't know whether their spending is effective, because they don't know what they're spending. And further, they lump things together, so that they may know the overall P&L for a period, but they don't know which activities and expenditures were working and which ones weren't. At Coke, we established P&Ls by brand—by month and in some cases by activity, and even by people. My premise was real simple: when you spend money you have to make money. And to know that, you have to do profit and loss statements, and you have to do them often.

When a Market's in Turmoil, Keep Spending

When a market is in turmoil, it's particularly important to have good, clear profit and loss statements. That's because you are going to have to decide at some point whether the market is suffering temporary problems or if it is going into a long-term decline and that you should get out. When a market, or an economy, goes into a tailspin, the first thing you should do is resist the temptation to cut spending. Not only should you keep

"When people are confused and don't know what to think, it's a great time for you to tell them."

spending in times of turmoil in order to keep from losing customers, but you should also realize that times of turmoil are
great growth opportunities.

For one thing, when people are confused and don't know
what to think, it's a great time for you to tell them. For another,
most of your competitors will probably cut spending when
things are unsettled, and that gives you the chance to increase
your market share.

In 1994, there was a devaluation in Mexico. I was skiing at
the time and was on the chairlift when someone said, "Mexico
devalued its currency." I got off the mountain as fast as I could
and called Coke's president, Doug Ivester, and told him that we
needed to get into Mexico because the operators there were
immediately going to try to cut marketing, and we were going
to end up destroying the business. He immediately agreed. We
knew that the Mexican public was going to be panicked by dramatic changes in their lives and personal economies. The
wealthy ones could no longer go to Houston to shop at the
Galleria shopping mall, and they couldn't drive foreign cars or
use American cellular phones because they suddenly had
become twice as expensive. The poorer ones would be worried
about eating.

We were no longer in a battle for share of market or share of
mind. We had entered into a battle of share of disposable income.
We were going to have to compete with every other product and
service in the Mexican marketplace; the idea was to get in and
make sure that consumers remembered to buy Coke.

Of course since the people operating our business in
Mexico were living through the same turmoil as everyone else,
we also knew that their immediate impulse was going to be to
cut back spending. So we came up with a plan to move money
around. We did cut some costs, but we maintained our highly
visible presence, and as a result in 1994, we actually grew
almost three times as fast as the market and competition. The
following year the business and our share of market also grew
radically because we stayed on the air, we talked to consumers
and told them why they should buy our product.

Yes, it was a scary strategy. And, yes, we did have to cut other expenses for a while. But because we had good profit and loss statements, we always knew exactly where we were and what was working and not working, so we could manage our way through the problem.

A great by-product of spending through times of turmoil is that it also allows you to put additional value into your product, which means that you can eventually charge more for it. What happens is that when people's finances are tight and they are worried, they will only buy the products that they think they can't live without. You want your product or service to make the cut, even if they can "literally" live without a product like Coke. In order to do this, you've got to keep talking to them. If you can get them to buy your product under less-than-ideal circumstances, you are convincing them that your product is very valuable. What happens next is that later, when times get better, they will have a residual sense of how much they value your product.

New Products Must Do Something New

When it comes to new products versus old products, I feel the same way that I feel about new markets versus old markets. The only reason to introduce new products is to make money. If

"New-product marketing for the sake of new-product marketing is lazy marketing."

you run the numbers and you think that you can increase your overall profit more by introducing a new product than by working harder to sell the old product, you should. But if you are worrying that you should introduce a new product just because your competitor has one, then you're thinking like a traditional marketer—and you're not going to maximize profits.

Don't assume that your competitor is smarter than you are or knows something that you don't. And don't be willing to help your competitor out by entering a stupid category along with him.

New-product marketing for the sake of new-product marketing is lazy marketing. You should only introduce new products if they will broaden your entry in a long-term category. New products have to capture growth that your current brand does not capture, or they have to enter new categories in the overall business, either directly or indirectly. And you shouldn't do it until you have decided that your existing products can no longer be stretched to address the needs and wants of more consumers (or more of the needs and wants of your current consumers).

New products do play a role in getting to a place that certain brands cannot go. I have already talked about the immune system of a brand. Obviously Coca-Cola Lemon is not going to be a huge seller, so if you want to participate in the lemon-lime category you need to introduce a lemon-lime product. Do you use the Coca-Cola trademark? The real issue there becomes whether the trademark has the flexibility to enter other categories. In the case of Coke and lemon-lime, the answer is no.

Whether you are introducing an entirely new brand such as Sprite or a line extension that builds on an existing brand, like Diet Coke, many of the issues are the same. Mainly you have to be sure that the new product does something distinctly different from what the old product can do. And at the same time you have to work to maintain the competitive position of your older product.

When You Have a New Product, Don't Ignore the Old Ones

One of the most celebrated line extensions of all times is Miller Lite. Beer drinkers as a group like to drink a lot of beer. Spending hours sharing brewskis with your buddies is part of the beer-drinking culture. In fact, one of the primary limitations on beer sales was that people got full after eight or ten of them

**"When (Miller) introduced Miller Lite,
everybody fell in love with it,
and they forgot about their other brands."**

and couldn't drink any more. So Miller concluded that it could sell more beer if it made a product that was less filling.

One approach would have been to redefine its attribute base, that is, to reposition its flagship Miller High Life brand to make it less filling than other beers. But Miller High Life was already a vibrant and popular brand. So Miller decided to introduce a lighter beer. With the famous campaign "Great Taste, Less Filling," Miller actually defined a cool, new category, and Miller Lite became the fastest growing brand in the category.

Unfortunately, what happened at Miller was that when they introduced Miller Lite, everybody in the company fell in love with it, and they forgot about their other brands. They had positioned Miller Lite as having this wonderful new trait of being less filling, but then they didn't do anything to tell consumers why they should keep drinking High Life. They also didn't do anything to tell consumers who didn't care about a less-filling beer why they should drink High Life instead of Budweiser, Heineken, or Corona. The introduction of Lite, like the introduction of any new product, had changed the makeup of the market, and Miller just ignored it. Imagine—they created the changes themselves and then didn't respond to them. Miller High Life, of course, went flat.

To make matters worse, while the people at Miller were busy patting themselves on the back for thinking up the whole new category of light beer, Anheuser-Busch came along and stole the market. Playing off of the strength of its Budweiser brand, it introduced Bud Light, while it also repositioned and grew Bud at the expense of Miller High Life. Of course, since Miller had already created the light category, Anheuser-Busch didn't have to do that. Miller had made great efforts to differentiate Lite from other beers, including High Life. But since the difference already existed in consumers' minds, Anheuser-Busch could take the opposite route of saying, "Hey, you can have a less filling beer that's also your old favorite, Budweiser." Bud Light became what I call the insurgent incumbent—it was the new guy on the block challenging the more established Miller Lite, but it had the power of the incumbency of Budweiser, America's favorite beer. And because the Miller folks were still reveling in their initial success, they didn't change tactics to fight back. As a result, when Anheuser-Busch told people: "Don't ask for a Lite, ask for a Bud Light," they did.

The Power of the Insurgent Incumbent

What Budweiser did with Bud Light is something that toothpaste makers do all the time. Whenever there is a new entry in the market or an improvement on an old product, they quickly extend their product lines to add the new features.

For many years, the big toothpaste battle was basically between Colgate and Crest. Colgate promised you white teeth, and Crest featured the American Dental Association seal of approval that backed up its claim to fight cavities. Then Close-Up came along as a gel and claimed that "we not only will make your teeth cleaner, we'll make your mouth taste fresher." It was a great proposition, and they got a big chunk of the market.

Soon Colgate and Crest jumped in with gels and promised all of their old attributes, plus the cleaning and refreshing quali-

**"There is infinite room to up the stakes,
and you have to make sure . . .
that you are the one who does it."**

ties of Close-Up. After that came the pump dispenser and Arm & Hammer's baking soda toothpaste. Each time, Procter & Gamble and Colgate matched the new entry. After playing the insurgent incumbent for years, however, Colgate has recently seized the offensive by combining all of the qualities, the gel and the baking soda, to come up with Colgate Total. It claims to fight cavities, freshen breath, reduce tartar, and fight gingivitis all at the same time. While the insurgent incumbent strategy is a good one if your competitor does happen to come up with a good idea, too many marketers think that that's enough. It isn't.

Ultimately, you have to take the initiative and set the stage. Don't just settle for being a player. No matter what your product or your market, no product ever attains perfection. There is always room to make teeth whiter, breath fresher, hair softer, and pain relief faster and more effective. There is infinite room to up the stakes, and you have to make sure that you are the one who does it.

The Volume Trap

Whether you do this through introducing new products or redefining your old products, the thing that you have to remem-

"New products can . . . bring in a lot of new volume but never make any money. But you must remember: you're not in the volume business, you're in the profit business."

ber is that you are in business to make money. The arguments that you hear most often for introducing new products are that they will stop a competitor or they will add volume. The most common argument against them is that you will cannibalize your old products. There are good arguments to be made for introducing or not introducing new products, but they aren't these. What the competitor does is important only if he is doing something that is taking business away from you or capturing new business that should be yours.

Volume alone is also a false issue. New products can be deceiving because they can bring in a lot of new volume but never make any money. But you must remember: you're not in the volume business, you're in the profit business. At Coke we had a great product called Fanta, yet Fanta was probably the most abused brand in the stable. Anytime we needed a new flavor, or better yet anytime that we needed to sell a couple of cases of product, we would introduce yet another flavor. Unfortunately, many of these flavors—like sarsaparilla, apple, raspberry—were inconsistent with the fundamental architecture of the brand. Fanta was basically a citrus brand. It was sharp and fun and was drunk mostly by kids. With the new flavors, we began to dilute the integrity and the identity of the brand. Sure, each of the new flavors would give us a quick hit in volume, but as we started looking at P&Ls by flavor, we came to the realization that even though we were getting volume, the overall profitability of the brand was deteriorating rapidly. If we didn't stop the erosion, eventually we were not going to make any money.

Look at what happened with all of the fast-food chains—McDonald's, Burger King and Wendy's—when they became too focused on volume. They all went out and built a bunch of stores and were delighted when more customers came through their doors. But they forgot that the cost of capital associated with carrying these assets was too high. When they started analyzing the economic value-add of these decisions, they realized that it was not adding value for the shareholders of the company but destroying it. Boston Chicken made the same mistake, only twice as bad—it built too many stores and also broadened its product definition too much when it became Boston Market.

It's easy to forget that incremental volume without profit isn't the issue—it's incremental profits through incremental volume that matter.

Make Sure Your Cannibals Eat Your Competitors

Worry about protecting your existing brands if you think that they are subject to cannibalization. But don't worry about launching a

"Cherry Coke. . . cannibalized our existing product Coca-Cola but was worthwhile because it took a greater toll on Pepsi."

new product because it may take volume from your old products. If your old products aren't strong enough to stand up to new competition, the companies that compete with you are going to figure that out soon enough. And if you're going to lose customers, you're better off losing them to another one of your product lines than to your competitor.

The key question in thinking about cannibalization is whether you are going to get a better return on all of your investments by introducing a new product or by broadening an old one. Often the best answer is to do both. The chances are that a new product is going to take some volume from your old products. What you need to do is to figure out if the new product is also going to take volume and/or profitability from your competitor or if it is going to grow the whole market so that there is more profitable volume for everyone. The important thing is to do rigorous consumer research and figure out before you act where the volume for the new product is going to come from and why. Then you have to decide if the returns you expect merit the investment.

Coca-Cola's introduction of Cherry Coke is a good example of a new product that cannibalized our existing product Coca-Cola but was worthwhile because it took a greater toll on Pepsi. Pepsi had set itself up as the product that was daring and exciting, while Coke's position in the market was more about reliability and comfort. So Cherry Coke was positioned as the naughty cousin of

Coke and ran ads showing people jumping out of airplanes. Given the positioning of Coke and Pepsi, the customers that it most appealed to were ones who were already drinking Pepsi. Sure, Classic Coke lost some customers, but Pepsi lost more, and The Coca-Cola Company ended up with more sales and profits.

T + A + CO = S, One Mexican's Marketing Recipe

Diet Coke, on the other hand, was a product whose strategy was to grow the overall market. The approach we used in deciding to launch Diet Coke was based on the elements that I later used in a model developed when I was a consultant and

"The Pepsi trademark was much larger than the Tab trademark and its success was greater."

called *TACOS. TACOS* stands for Trademark + Area + Consumer Offering = Success. What it means is that the size of your trademark as compared to that of your competition, plus the size of the area of business in which you are going to compete, plus the size of your consumer offering or unique selling proposition is going to be the size of your success. We tested this by arguing that Diet Coke was a better idea than Tab.

Tab was a very small trademark. It was a trademark that was known but not very appealing. It competed in the hard-core diet category, which at the time was a medium-size category with about ten percent of the soft-drink market. Tab's unique selling proposition was figure maintenance and calorie control, and it had about a 4 percent share of the soft-drink market. Pepsi had two entries in the area, Diet Pepsi and Pepsi Light, which had a hint of lemon. The two products together were larger than Tab, with a 4.1 percent share of the market.

We looked at the situation and saw that for Pepsi, the *A*, the area of business, was the same as Tab, and the *CO*, the consumer offering of figure maintenance and calorie control, was the same. But the Pepsi trademark was much larger than the Tab trademark and its success was greater. So we decided to replace the Tab trademark in the diet category with the Coke trademark and to come up with a new consumer offering that would appeal to more people.

The Coke trademark was the largest trademark in the soft-drink business. It was a huge *T* that promised much better success than the small *T* position that Tab had. The area of the business was the same ten percent, but we projected that if Diet Coke entered, the area was going to be significantly larger. And in the consumer-offering arena, we decide to move away from calories and go for a taste offering. The unique selling proposition of Diet Coke was that you were going to drink it just for the taste of it. This was made possible in part by the promise of additional sweetening systems that were going to change the landscape of the diet market. With the larger trademark and the larger consumer offering, we figured that the area of business would grow significantly, as would our success. So, we settled on a projection that Diet Coke alone would win a ten percent share or an amount equal to the total diet category at that time.

Our plan was for that market to double and for us to take a fifty percent share. As a result, Diet Coke ended up with a market share two and a half times that of Tab.

The dry beer phenomenon is another good *TACOS* example. Dry was a product that actually had more alcohol in it than regular beer, and was first introduced by Sapporo as Super Dry in Japan. In the United States, Bud went to market first, with a brand called Bud Dry, and Miller was considering it aggressively. At the time, I was working with Miller, so we ran the *TACOS* model on it. What we figured was that the Miller brand was about half the size in relative terms of the Bud brand. The dry category is very, very small, so we were going to enter a very small category, and we didn't have much of a unique selling proposition. So when we added it up, a small trademark, in a small category, and with a small consumer proposition, Miller couldn't make any money, and in a very smart move decided not to enter it. This decision, in turn, did not validate Bud Dry and contributed to the fading of the whole category.

While ignoring the competition and refusing to enter a market can sometimes be the right strategy, at other times, you need to enter a market to control the dialogue, even if the market doesn't seem to make any sense. I have already talked about Crystal Pepsi and how Coke countered with Tab Clear to hijack the dialogue and force Pepsi's sugared product to compete in the diet category. When we sufficiently fuzzed up the issues and confused the customers so that the market died, we considered it a great success. Similarly, at Miller, if we had looked at Bud Dry from a different perspective, we might have decided to divert Anheuser-Busch's attention and resources from the big Bud brand into the tiny Bud Dry brand. Not only was it the right decision for Miller, but it was a decision that was made based on P&L facts and a premeditated strategy, rather than as a knee-jerk response to the activities of a competitor.

Find the S.O.B.

Underlying everything I've been saying in this chapter, in fact everything I have said and will say in this book, is that you should never take your eye off of the bottom line. Everything

> **"You have to figure out what people are going to stop buying if they start buying your new product."**

you do, whether it's deciding to enter a new market or not to enter it, whether it's launching a new product or not launching one, needs to be made in response to the fundamental question: Where am I going to get the best return on my investment and make the most money? And to arrive at that answer, I always think about the S.O.B.

No, it doesn't stand for what you think. S.O.B. stands for Source Of Business. Who is going to buy your product and where are they going to get the money? When you are introducing a new product, you have to figure out what people are going to stop buying if they start buying your new product. In a way, you are dealing with a zero sum game.

Occasionally, new products will create whole new markets, as computers did. And sometimes a new product can lead to the expansion of a market, as Diet Coke did. But even if a new product is going to grow the market, at least initially the new volume is probably going to come out of someone's old volume. This means that you have to ask yourself if what you are proposing to offer will really be more attractive to consumers than what's already available to them. And if it is, which product is going to lose out? Yours? Or someone else's?

Even products that seem entirely new, like Post-it notes, take their business from somewhere else. Post-its opened up a whole new behavior and a whole new market, but it actually replaced the pad of paper on which you took notes with a more efficient way. The product broadened the definition and use, but it made obsolete something that was in place.

Fishing where the fish are should also be part of your S.O.B. thinking, because even if there's a huge potential for your product, and even if you find consumers willing and in need of your product, if they don't have the cash, they won't be able to buy it. Look for the countries where there is disposable income. Look at the politics and the economic models. Is the government committed to a market-based economy? What are the prospects for growth in GDP and GNP? What are the prospects that economic growth will translate into more wealth and disposable income for lots of people? You must build these into your models to ensure that your projections are doable based not only on the willingness and desire of consumers to buy your product, but also on a viable, economic perspective.

It's amazing how many marketers don't think about these things. They get excited about some new item that they think is going to pull a rabbit out of a hat and give them a blockbuster season, and they just go for it, without really thinking it through. So, if nothing else, this is just a reminder: think about where the business is going to come from because it will help you ground your brand and allow you to figure out what you need to do in order to have the most relevance in the market.

Think about All the Potential Growth

I used to think that the goal of a marketer should be to capture all of the growth in a market—the organic growth, the growth created by the economy, the growth created by your competi-

> **"Taco Bell . . . came up with a whole new potential market and a great new proposition."**

tion, and the growth created by you. If you do this, your share of market will naturally grow. But I've decided that this goal isn't ambitious enough. If you really want to maximize your profits, you need to capture the potential growth as well. Of course, that's a theoretical goal that you can never achieve, but aiming for it is important because it helps you to think about things in new and productive ways.

Mainly, it makes you think about exactly what the potential market is and what you are competing against. If you're selling soft drinks in Japan, you are competing against green tea and coffee. In Ireland, you are competing against beer. In Russia and some of the developing economies, you are competing against candy bars and magazines and other things that people might buy with just a bit of spare money. And in India and other poor economies, you are competing against everything.

One of the best examples of how this kind of competitive evaluation pays off is Taco Bell. When Taco Bell started out, it was positioned in the general market for Mexican food. Its potential customers were people who actively liked Mexican food, and the people who bought it occasionally as a change of pace. The product defined the market—tacos as opposed to burgers or pizza. The problem was that this put it in competition with all the other Mexican restaurants, including many that had much better food, and the market overall wasn't that big.

But when Taco Bell took another look and reconsidered its competition, it came up with a whole new potential market and a great new proposition. The competition wasn't Pedro's Cantina down the street, but McDonald's, Burger King, KFC, and everybody else in the fast-food business. Then Taco Bell proceeded to redefine the experience of fast food on the basis of ease of use and price. They introduced a forty-nine-cent taco, gave consumers a new idea of what a quick meal should be, and actually changed the makeup of the market. You have probably experienced the benefit of this attack on the part of Taco Bell, because the overall price of a hamburger dropped as a result.

Growth Is the Goal

At the end of the day, growth is the goal and the imperative. Introducing anything or doing any kind of tactical activity that

"Doing (anything) . . . that doesn't create growth is just not worth the trip."

doesn't create growth is just not worth the trip. Anyone who studies, reads, or tries to educate himself or herself is trying to grow. It's the same with making money. When you are trying to make more money, you are trying to grow. Anytime someone walks into your office and says, "We have to defend our position in the market," fire them. Anytime your advertising agency says, "We're going to stem the decline of the brand," fire them. Go hire people who have the idea and the vision that growing is the only way to go. If you don't grow, what will happen is what happens to us as human beings—if you don't grow, you die.

How do you do this, how do you grow? The first thing you need to do is look for where the opportunities are. How do you redefine your brand, how do you redefine your market? Where do you find the equivalent of that manicure on Virgin Airways in your soap, cigarette, soft drink, or beer? Where do you find a smoother ride in a car and how do you translate that into the brand that you're selling? How do you find Sony Triniton, or how do you find the Intel Inside that defines products in a whole different way? How do you look for things that are not obvious? Sometimes the answers to these questions will take you into new markets. Once you have saturated your existing markets, you have to move into new areas. But you have to have a balanced approach to new and existing markets. Go ahead and open a new territory or build in new cities, but never do that at the expense of sacrificing the opportunity and profitability of those existing markets with your existing brands.

Marketing cannot be isolated from economics, politics, or anything else that is going on in the world. Marketing is business, and that means that you must take into account whether you can make and sell the product, and whether consumers can buy the product. This means that you have to consider technology, economics, accounting, finance, and government, as well as culture, demographics, and history. Unless you look at all of these things and think about how they are going to change and affect tomorrow, you will continue to live in the past, and you will be launching brands that will end up in the cemetery of bad ideas. They will be grounded in tactics and not in destination, and you will never survive.

However, if you keep looking and thinking about all the

factors that will have a deep influence on how your product is going to perform, then, unequivocally, you will be successful. You will have the most relevant brand in the marketplace because you will understand the competition and why it is relevant, and why consumers are attracted to that brand or product or idea. You'll be able to offer them something that is different, better, and special, and you'll be able to take an idea in an organic way to more and more markets around the world. If you do this, you will make a lot of money, shareholders will be happy, and you will be very successful.

8

DON'T STOP THINKING ABOUT TOMORROW

Maybe the goal of religious mystics is to live purely in the present, but a marketer always has to be planning what he or she is going to do tomorrow. That's because no matter what you have done to get you to where you are today, you are going to have to do something different tomorrow. No matter how successful you've been, there's no resting on your laurels.

Before and during the 1996 Olympics, everybody in Atlanta was fixated on the games and the preparations. Since Coke was a major sponsor, a lot of people in the company were involved in planning the opening ceremonies or brainstorming about who would carry the torch at the end. But while they were doing that, my concern was recovery. I was thinking about the day after the games ended. Once the hoopla of the Olympics and the attendant advertising blitzes were over, what were we going to do next? How was The Coca-Cola Company going to maintain and grow its business without the boost from the games? How could we use the excitement surrounding Coke and the Olympics going into the next year?

Getting people to think realistically about tomorrow is hard. The present is so exciting, and dreaming about the future is fun. But actually getting down to dealing with the nitty-gritty reality that tomorrow is going to bring is tough. In part, this is because the future seems so unpredictable. And, of course, it's true that you can't know in advance how tomorrow is going to turn out.

But it's also true that if you work at it, you can have some input.

You have to constantly be thinking and planning for the future, because if you don't, when it arrives you will be unprepared, and it will engulf you.

Planning and pushing to grab hold of tomorrow before it gets here are what everybody in business *must* do. If you want to get ahead, you can't be attached to the past or the present. You have to let go and step out into the unknown.

At Coke, we had some countries that planned for the day after the Olympics, and others that just wouldn't even think about it. Guess what happened? The ones with a plan kept on selling, while the ones without a plan went into a slump. Heck, one country, a pretty big one, even believed that because the retailers, wholesalers, and the rest of the trade had given us so much feature activity as a result of the games, they would now ignore Coke and give the competition a chance. That's ridiculous. The reason that the trade gave us the features and display activity is because we gave them reasons to feature us. If we kept giving them reasons, they would continue to feature us.

What happens to your product in the market today definitely depends on how well you prepared yesterday, or last month, or last year.

The Future Is Coming—Don't Wait for It

Implicit in preparing for the future is the notion that things are going to change. And because change is scary, a lot of people prefer not to think about it. "Well, let's wait and see what happens," they'll say. Or, "Things are going well, so why should we

---

"Things are going to change tomorrow. So either you can be the one who changes them or somebody will change them for you."

---

worry?" I understand the reasoning that if you wait for more information, you'll reduce the risk of doing something disastrously wrong. Unfortunately, it also reduces your success because it means that you are always playing catch-up. You know that whether things are going well or poorly, things are going to change tomorrow. So either you can be the one who changes them or somebody will change them for you.

It's funny that on one level, people clearly know that they have to plan. All you need to do to see that is to try to get an appointment on some executive's calendar. You may have to wait two months because he or she has scheduled every day with meetings, conferences, plant visits, investor presentations, and whatever. If you asked any CEO in America what he or she is doing next Friday, I'm willing to bet that he or she would not say, "I don't have any plans. I haven't thought about it." However, if you asked what he or she expects to happen as a result of the meetings on Friday and what exactly the company is going to do to get where it needs to be sixty days hence, you're very unlikely to get a clear answer. That's just not smart business.

Create the Future

Think of how Starbucks changed the market for coffee by redefining its uses, and how computer makers are coming up with new ways for people to use PCs. When you think about

---

"Every time you change the definition of yourself, you put your competitors, by comparison, in a totally different position."

---

the future, you have to think about how it is going to unfold if you just sit and watch or just keep doing what you've always been doing. You also have to think about ways that you can change it to your advantage. This is particularly important, because by defining and redefining yourself, you can constantly move away from your competitors. Every time you change the definition of yourself, you put your competitors, by comparison, in a totally different position.

But redefining yourself doesn't just affect the comparative positioning of your competitors. It also changes your customers and your relationship with them.

I'm not advocating in any way that you throw away what works. You *should* keep on doing what works, but you also have to add to it to ensure that things continue to work.

You should strive to do what Arm & Hammer did with baking soda by coming up with a product and saying, "Hey, you know who we are. You know that this is a good product and you think you know all of the uses of baking soda. Here are two hundred more uses for this product. Put an open box in the refrigerator. This will remind you to use it in something you are baking, and then while it's sitting there it will be deodorizing your fridge, so you need to throw it out after thirty days."

I think that the McIlhennys, who make Tabasco, should think about this. Every cupboard in the world has a bottle of Tabasco in it. The problem is that nobody uses much of it. They need to come up with some new uses and remind people that you can put it in the food while you are cooking it and on the food after you have cooked it. Maybe you can do other things with it as well. Maybe it cleans metal pans, or keeps away bugs. I don't know. But then, it's not my job to know. It's the job of the Tabasco people to know and to tell me. They need to change their relationship with me by giving me new reasons to use their product.

Change Begets More Change

When you do this, however, you have to remember that every time you change, you are creating conditions that are going to require that you change again. Consumers will buy your prod-

"Once they've acted on the reasons you give them today, you will have, in essence, created a new consumer."

uct if you give them reasons to. But once they've acted on the reasons you give them today, you will have, in essence, created a new consumer.

Last month, for example, you may have had a consumer who drank Coke whenever he or she was thirsty, wanted to be refreshed, or was eating a hamburger. This meant that they consumed about eight Cokes a week. Say this month, you tell them that drinking Coke is also a sociable thing to do, and that boosts their consumption to ten Cokes a week. Now, when next month comes, you are going to have a consumer who is already drinking Coke anytime they are thirsty, want to be refreshed, are eating a hamburger, or want to be sociable. So if you want them to drink more than ten Cokes a week, you are going to have to give them more reasons. The new reason that worked this month isn't going to work next month because the consumer will have developed some immunity to it—you tried it, it worked, now he or she is expecting something better yet. He or she has already factored in this month's reason, and now needs another new one. Consumption, definition, redefinition, and reinvention are the essence of growth.

Similarly, when the political or the economic landscapes change, as they constantly do, you have to adapt your marketing efforts to the new circumstances. You can't just sit around and say, "Boy, we really had a good year last year, hence we are going to have a good year next year." That just isn't in the cards.

Think about what happened last year in the world—1998 was a year of tremendous change. It was a year in which new presidents were elected in half a dozen countries. Latin America changed altogether. We had the Asian crisis. We had the Mexican and Brazilian problems. We had currency devaluations. We had unemployment go away and come back. Interest rates went up and then went down. The market climbed to new highs, crashed, and then climbed to new highs again. All of this is going to have an effect on how consumers behave, and unless you take that into account, and change what you are doing, you will never get to where you want to be.

Sometimes your destination, in terms of percentage share of the market, or growth of volume, or whatever, may not change, but sometimes it will, or it should. As the future unfolds, new opportunities will open up. Or maybe you can even open them up.

Different Plans Need Different Resources

Whether you decide to keep your old destination or to come up with a new one, you always have to be thinking about how you are going to get there. Is the future a forty percent share? Is the

---

"Once you decide what you want the future to be, you have to create the tools necessary to get you there."

---

future twenty percent growth over what you are today? Is your future a healthy one? Once you decide what you want the future to be, you have to create the tools necessary to get you there.

If you figure out that you are going to cross the river and you don't have a boat, you are going to have to build either a pontoon or a bridge, or go buy or rent a boat to get to the other side. If you just stand at the edge of the river and say, "Hey, I think I'm going to hang here and see what happens," you will watch the world go by.

And when you are thinking about the tools and tactics you

are going to need in the future, you also need to think about the people and the skills that you have available. The reason for this is that the skills necessary to get you here are not necessarily the same skills that you will need to get to the next level. You know you need a set of skills and a specific physical condition to run a ten-kilometer race. Let me tell you, running a ten-kilometer race doesn't mean that you can run a marathon. Climbing to five thousand feet on a mountain doesn't mean that you can climb Mount Everest right away. Being successful today does not mean that you are going to be successful tomorrow. You are going to have to develop a whole new set of skills, or you might need to hire people who have a whole different set of skills than the ones that you had before.

You cannot bank on yesterday's success. You can't just say, "Heck, everything is going well today," because one happy day everything will fall apart. It's happening in companies everywhere—and by the time you realize that your business is not growing anymore, it's too late.

I always assume that tomorrow's going to be worse than today from a business perspective, and then I plan to make it better. David Stern, the commissioner of the NBA, once paid me a fabulous compliment. He said that most people look at a glass as half full or half empty, but that I look at the glass and say it's broken, and that we need to make a new one and *then* fill it up. The way I see it is that I'm always running scared, and planning for that inevitability that things won't be as good tomorrow as they are today. In order to ensure the success of your product or service, you should do the same.

Break Your Own Rules

The only way to grab hold of the future is by fundamentally challenging yourself. You have to continually challenge your own concept, your own brand, your own ideas.

I actually think it's funny as hell when people start talking about breaking the rules, because they almost always assume that the rules belong to someone else. But the fact is, once you start

"The game is to constantly change the definition of what you are doing, so that your competition is constantly lagging behind."

working with a group or team of people, you adjust and embrace the rules that apply to that operation, that army, that country, that political party, that brand, that company. Therefore, in order to break the rules, you've got to question your own concepts or ideas.

Most people are afraid of breaking rules, so you must encourage people to challenge and change the very things that made them successful in the first place. If you don't do this, you can bet that somebody else will swoop in and gladly make whatever it was that you should've made obsolete obsolete. With this one act, they will be capturing the future and moving ahead of you.

If you're already successful, the biggest problem you are going to encounter is that you have become the marketing captain for your category. You know that your competitors are not stupid. If you are eating their lunch, your competitors are going to start looking at you and gravitating toward the things that are working for you. So you always have to be thinking of the next new thing that you are going to do.

I have a friend who bought one of those Sony Vaio notebook computers as soon as it came on the market. She told me how great it was because it was so light, and that she bought it because it was the only one that fit so easily into her briefcase and her backpack. You know what? It took only three months for Toshiba to come up with one just like it. Why? Fundamentally because products are getting more and more generic. The components of computers, Internet providers, soft drinks, and cigarettes, the basics for all of these are generic. People can imitate you very quickly.

How long does it take for someone to copy a commercial?

When one company starts using polar bears or frogs in its commercials, how long does it take for everyone to start using animals in their advertising? How long does it take for everybody to start using humor after one guy does it successfully?

The captains of the category are the leaders. The successful ones are those who actually change the definition of what they are, but unfortunately the cycle time in which those ideas remain original is getting shorter and shorter.

To succeed in the future, you must not only operate your own business but you must also think about what you want your competition to do. Before you decide to sponsor something, for example, think about how your competitors will counteract. Like chess or poker, you're basically saying, "See you and raise you and raise you again." The endgame is to constantly change the definition of what you are doing, so that your competition is constantly lagging behind.

Zero-Base Your Thinking

Momentum doesn't just happen. I know from a pure physics standpoint, that sentence makes no sense, because momentum

"I say to myself, what if I were just entering this market?"

is supposed to be a force that keeps you in motion, but in marketing, the fact is that you constantly need to be doing something to make momentum happen.

To get ahead of everybody else, you will need to accelerate that momentum with propulsion. You constantly need a strong and steady stream of new marketing ideas and reasons why consumers should buy your product or service.

Now, how do you do this? I have always been successful at this by using the principle that you must zero-base your thinking. By this, I mean that I am constantly rethinking what is going on with my brand or product, or what is going on in the marketplace. I look at the information I have about the behavior of consumers, sales, and the reactions of my competition, and I say to myself, What if I were just entering this market?

When I was with Coke, I would think about relaunching Coke every day. What if I had a brand that was new but enjoyed all the equity that the Coke brand had? How would I launch it? How would I position it in the marketplace? If you had a brand-new airline and you were American Airlines, how would you launch a brand-new airline that already had a large fleet of planes, the big distribution network, huge equity with consumers, and a frequent-flyer program? If you are Procter & Gamble and you dominate the detergent business, what kind of detergent would you introduce in order to make your own brand obsolete? How would you make Tide obsolete? When you think of things this way, you will find new ways of going to the future and of creating new products and environments that are advantageous to you and not advantageous for your competition.

Recently, Bill Bradley, a former senator from New Jersey, said he was thinking about running for president. I thought that a great platform for him would be for him to say, "I had to get out of government to look at government. I've been out looking at it from the outside, and I am truly an outsider. Now, having been in government and having been out, I understand exactly what it is that needs to be done." I actually like this positioning because this is what I did in business. I left Coca-Cola in 1986 and went out and learned a lot. I worked for many different companies, and went to places I had never been before. I zero-based my thinking and threw away, temporarily, everything I knew. I said: What if I could reset my brain to zero, and load it with a whole new set of information on the basis of what's here, and then blend that information with the existing programs that I have saved in my memory? What would happen? How would this hybrid thinking look?

When I went back to Coke, I had a hybrid of information. This was the combination of resetting my brain to zero, learning from all of those new experiences with people and companies that had never been involved with the soft-drink business, and then blending it with what I had learned before. Sure, I remembered many of the things we had done before, but I was constantly coloring my thinking with the things I learned on the outside. I left again in 1998, and today I find myself doing exactly the same thing. It is a process that allows me to forget what I knew and forces me to see things in ways I never have before.

Today, I am working on selling cement, prefab housing, and energy to residential customers. The reason I picked these industries and these customers is because I am trying to find new industries and forums that will challenge my thinking as I go into the future. You know, every time I do this, I end up with really good ideas. Exposing yourself to today's new and different industries and experiences really changes and evolves your thinking. It is like the Italian Renaissance, taking all the good from yesterday and blending it with the best of today's new ideas to come up with something prettier, nicer, and more successful or fruitful.

Once you do this, you need to get consumers to look at your brands with a new, fresh point of view as well. We did this at Coke by managing the imagery of the brand, by sponsoring something new, by saying something new about the brand, by changing the packaging, by having commercials that appealed to different people, and by running promotions that appealed to whatever psyche consumers had at that time and whatever was affecting them. We constantly redefined the brand.

Basically, we created the brand in front of consumers, involving them and drawing them into it rather than chasing after them with a proposition that might not have worked.

Your brand needs to lead the consumer so that he or she will aspire to your proposition. When you do this, they will find more value in your brand and want to buy it. They will be excited and refreshed by your point of view. Guess what? They'll buy your stuff more often in more places more times, and you'll make more money.

Kill Last Year's Ideas

An essential element of inventing and reinventing is creativity. Creativity is one of those magical, mystical words that marketing

---

"While creativity does mean changing from what was done in the past, it doesn't mean criticism of what was done in the past."

---

people throw around a lot when they want to avoid responsibility for producing results. But the truth is that creativity, like everything else in marketing, is not some unpredictable force of nature. It can be managed. You just have to understand what it is that you are doing and what it is that you are trying to accomplish when you are being creative.

The first thing you have to understand is that creativity is by definition destructive. People focus on the constructive part of creativity, the fact that somebody constructs a new concept or a new widget. But inherent in the concept is also the fact that every time you come up with a new idea or widget, you are superseding or destroying an existing idea or widget. In a way, creativity is a process of disinventing. This means that being creative requires having the courage to say, "Hey, that was my idea, and it was a good idea then, but it is no longer a good idea. This new idea, which replaces that one, is a lot better for the current time." The reason that it's important to understand this is that it explains why people say that they like creativity but are in fact are so reluctant to take responsibility for it. What they don't like about creativity and the reason that they shy away from it is that they don't want to be seen as complainers and critics.

So, what you have to remember is that while creativity does mean changing from what was done in the past, it doesn't mean criticism of what was done in the past. It's not about saying that your idea is better than anyone else's. Rather, it is about moving into the future and inventing something that you understand will inevitably be made obsolete in the future by yet another creative idea. The commercials of this year will be made obsolete by the commercials of next year. That's a fact of life. If you're concerned that the guy who had your job before is going to be offended by this, get over it. Somebody else is going to be sitting in your place next year.

When I left Coke, I had a lot of very good friends in the marketing department, and over the last few months, I've heard them say, "Oh, things are not the same." My answer to them is, "Of course they're not. They're different, but times are different. You have to believe that what you have today is better for today." You must look at the current environment as the new environment in which you live, and you have to strive to create, invent, and grow. It's not about being better, bigger, or smaller, it is just different. In that environment you will have an opportunity to do all of the things you can to be extraordinarily successful.

Learn to Manage Creativity

Once you get over your probably unacknowledged fear of creativity, you can start managing it to accomplish what you want and need. As I have said many times, you have to have a desti-

"If you just say, 'Let's have a creative session,' you'll find that ninety percent of what people come up with is garbage."

nation. And once you have a destination, you can target creativity toward reaching it.

I like to say that creativity is like a divining rod. You don't know where you are going to find water, but when you use a divining rod, you do know that you are looking for water and not oil. With creativity, you have to be specific about what it is you are trying to be creative about. Are you trying to reinvent a product? Are you trying to launch a new way of manufacturing something? Are you trying to change a package? You must decide beforehand what your goal is.

If you don't, if you just say, "Let's have a creative session," you'll find that ninety percent of what people come up with is garbage. The reason for this is that if nobody sets up at the beginning of the session what it is you are looking for, people will suffer from a lack of direction. Before every executive session, I write a brief that says exactly what we need to do. I lay out our strategy and the positioning we want, or the goal we are trying to achieve. Then I ask, "Now what are the things that we can say or do differently to achieve that goal?"

In a later chapter, I will talk about advertising agencies and the reason that I changed Coca-Cola's relationship with ad agencies. At the heart of the switch, however, was the fact that I felt that I owned the positioning of the products and that I needed to set the destination that Coca-Cola wanted to reach. Then it was the advertising agencies' job to find creative ways to accomplish what I wanted done. In the old days, the agencies felt that they could just be creative without any direction from me.

Anyhow, once you have written your brief stating what you are trying to accomplish, then you manage the creativity by testing the ideas that everyone comes up with against whether or not they help you reach your goal. Be prepared for the fact that people will probably come up with ideas you don't particularly like. Hell, even the person coming up with the idea might not even like it, but it doesn't really make any difference. If it helps accomplish the objective, it is a good idea. If it doesn't, toss it out and look for another one.

I went to an agency session once after I left Coca-Cola, and this guy had written this brilliant paper that outlined the strategic direction that the company should follow. The agency, which I like and respect very much, had actually participated and collaborated in writing this paper. Then the creative guy with the earring and the pajamas gets up and says, "Okay, here is the creative." I sat there and thought, "Whatever happened from the brief to the creative?" The guy said, "Well this is really good creative." I said, "I agree, I think the idea is beautiful. The problem is, it doesn't fit with your goal, which was stated in the brief."

If you use strategy and discipline, in the process of managing creativity, you can get the results that you want.

Keep Moving the Finish Line

Another point to remember is that a destination is nothing more than a new starting point. People like to say that "today is the beginning of the future," but they often don't act that way. The truth is: anytime you're working on reaching your current desti-

> **"Anytime you're working on reaching your current destination, you have to start thinking about what your next destination is."**

nation, you have to start thinking about what your next destination is.

How long does it take to figure out where you are going next and how to get there? It takes a ton of time. I always had arguments with the advertising agencies that we worked with at Coke because they would often finish a bunch of commercials and then want to take six months off to rest. My argument was, "You know, we've just finished producing the best ideas that you've ever had. Now you need to start working on creating new ones right away so we can be ready six months from now. If you start six months from now, we're not going to be ready until a year from now. If you don't start right now, it will be too late when I need it."

The same principle applies to all of your plans. When do you start planning for the next year? Now. Start planning for next February at the end of this February. And once you know the results from this year, use them to plan for next year. And you can't use the same old techniques—you have to find new ways of appealing to consumers so that you can grow even more.

Even though it's important to keep moving the finish line, it is important to define small victories, and enjoy them. You could argue that the concept of focusing on a destination doesn't allow for small victories along the way. But, as a matter of fact, it does. If you are training for a marathon, your ultimate goal is to run those 26.2 miles. But, if you just look at that gruesome distance and how much you are going to hurt, you will drop out of the race. So you have to enjoy the small victory you get every day when you make it through another training session. You can't celebrate so hard that you decide that you don't still have to accomplish more. But you need to keep up your morale. In business, maybe it's a promotion that worked really well. Maybe it's a commercial that moved the needle. Maybe it's the successful hiring of a coveted executive. All these steps move you toward the destination, and you should celebrate them as victories along the way.

Little Steps Can Take You a Long Way

Sometimes creativity results in your doing new things, like coming up with a new positioning for your product. Coke used to be positioned as the melancholic brand, the one that the coach gave to kids after they lost their baseball game. Today we have

"Creativity is more like ten yards in a cloud of dust. It is a ground game."

expanded the positioning to say that Coke is also refreshing and energetic, and it tastes good and a million other things. To communicate this positioning there are polar bears, Christmas caravans, and people with track shoes running around in the desert, and packages that have the bottle on it. All of these things are creative ways to help communicate a broader positioning statement and to ask consumers to drink the product more often in more places so that the company can make more money.

But creativity isn't just about finding new things to do. It is also helpful in finding new and better ways to do the things that you are already doing. Year after year, Budweiser keeps telling people that "This Bud's for you." But they used to do it with a bunch of muscular, blue-collar workers. Today they are selling beer with frogs.

People often think of creativity as involving a big breakthrough idea, of being a Hail Mary play that dramatically wins the game. But that's not the case. Just as often, perhaps more often, creativity is more like ten yards in a cloud of dust. It is a ground game. It is a small increment of the thought and presentation and the explanation of why I should buy a product or fly an airline or drive a car or eat a candy bar. It is that little thing that says, "Oh yeah, here is one more reason why I should do it."

I actually suspect that there may be a lot of good big ideas out there, but most people find them too scary to seriously consider. Therefore, I think that you need to consciously approach creativity and the search for new ideas the same way that you approach traveling for pleasure. When you plan a trip overseas, you prepare yourself to learn and discover. After all, that's why you are going on the trip. I think that you need to do the same thing in business. If you understand that creative new ideas will take you places that you haven't been before, then you will embrace them rather than cringe. And if you remain grounded in your strategy, you can step out boldly and seize the future before it gets here.

Always remember: if you change before you have to, by the time the competition catches up to you, you will already be someplace else.

PART 3

WITH WHOSE ARMY?

9

DON'T COUNT PEOPLE– COUNT RESULTS

So now I've given you a long list of what I think it takes to be a successful marketer. You have to:

Pick a destination so that you will know where you are trying to go.

Develop strategies about how you are going to reach the destination.

Figure out where you want to position your product in the minds of consumers.

Create brands and images for those brands.

Understand customers.

Constantly sell your product by giving them more and more reasons to buy it.

Invent brands.

Go to new markets.

Grow in existing markets.

Creatively think about packaging, promotions, distribution, and advertising.

Constantly test and measure the results of everything that you do.

Continually refresh your brands and strategies to maximize not only current sales but also future sales.

And finally, you have to do it in lots of different markets.

By now, you are probably thinking, "And with whose army am I going to do this? You just told me to buy a hundred horses, but who is going to ride them? You told me to get a fleet of airplanes, but where am I going to get the pilots? You told me to do destination planning—but how am I going to get this done? Who is going to do it? There's only one of me!"

Well, the answer is that you need to build a marketing organization, and you need to fill it with good people, lots of them.

When I worked at Coke the first time, I was always frustrated because I had a lot of ideas, but I didn't have enough people to carry them out. I saw the same thing when I left Coke. In many companies, there were good ideas all over the place that would probably have sold lots of product, but they were not getting implemented just because there weren't enough people. So when I went back to Coke, I kept this mental image in my mind: there are five hundred buses sitting in the parking lot with nobody to drive them. All of the buses are ready, the routes are ready, gas is in the tanks, but there are no drivers. It focused me on doing what I had to do to hire the people I needed.

The future of marketing lies in establishing it as a professional discipline that is based on sound business principles and that produces sound business results.

There are two essential reasons for this. One is that, as I hope I have shown in the past few chapters, when you use sound business principles in your approach to marketing, the marketing that you produce is much more effective. The other is that only by clearly establishing that marketing is a sound business investment that produces clear and measurable results can marketers ever get the kind of resources that they need to do their jobs effectively. As long as marketing is viewed as a nonessential activity, and therefore an expense, executives will feel free to randomly cut marketing budgets. This reduces its effectiveness and invites further cuts. It is a downward spiral to oblivion.

Hire Professionals, Not Amateurs

Marketing is not just some fluffy optional activity, but rather it is a key strategic discipline that must be approached in a system-

> **"Really wanting a job won't do it.**
> **They have to love marketing and want**
> **to eat, drink, breathe, and sleep marketing."**

atic and professional manner. And to do that, you're going to have to become much more disciplined about hiring and developing professional marketing staffs.

There are a lot of very good marketers who have become professionals through years of apprenticeship. I count myself as one of them. My first job was as a brand assistant with Procter & Gamble in Mexico working on the Ariel detergent brand. After a year or so, I moved up to being a salesman, then I came back to work as a brand manager on Crest, and then Safeguard. Later the New York ad agency McCann-Erickson offered me a job, so I went to work on the Coca-Cola account in Mexico. That led to other assignments, such as living in Japan working on the Nestlé and General Motors accounts, and then to New York to work on a Coca-Cola Bottling account. Eventually, PepsiCo (yes, PepsiCo!) hired me as head of marketing in Brazil. Then they sent me to New York, where I was the director of marketing for Pepsi in the United States, and later I joined Coca-Cola in Atlanta.

Whew.

When I started out, I didn't know anything about marketing. I became a marketer because Procter & Gamble needed people in marketing and they were willing to hire me.

This unfortunately is an all-too-common occurrence. Because executives don't really understand marketing, they hire whatever bodies come along, or dump their brothers-in-law and the other people they don't know what to do with, into the marketing department. Fortunately some of them, especially the young kids who have the energy and the desire to learn, do a good job despite their initial lack of qualifications. But companies also end up with a lot of people in jobs for which they aren't qualified.

In the past, in a less competitive environment, you could get by with just a few good marketers and a bunch of other people to answer the telephone and shepherd projects. But in the future, you aren't going to be able to get away with that. Every day, marketers have to do more and more and work harder and smarter to convince more customers to buy their products rather than the other guy's. That means you need a lot of people, and every one of them has to carry a full load.

You need their knowledge and brainpower to come up with smart plans, and their discipline and hands-on skills to carry them out. If companies want to sell more stuff, they need more marketing professionals to do it. And they need to make sure that they have the right mix of talents to do everything better than the competition does. If you want to play in the big leagues, you've got to create a team of professionals.

The issue of getting appropriate resources really comes to the forefront when it comes to staffing. Once you start talking about hiring an army of the best and the brightest marketers in the world, the dollar signs are going to light up in your employer's eyes, and the financial guys are going to step in and say there is a head count freeze. In order to win the ensuing hiring-budget battle, a marketer has to do two things.

The first is that you need to realize, and to convince your boss, that marketing is a profession.

Marketers are professionals with specific skills that you need to find and pay for. You cannot just hire Cousin Vinnie's son and put him in marketing because he needs a job. You can't hire somebody because he says, "Hey, I'm a consumer. I buy stuff. And I know a lot of people who buy stuff, so I know how to market." People are not born marketers. They have to learn to be marketers, and they have to really want to be marketers.

Really wanting a job won't do it. They have to love marketing and want to eat, drink, breathe, and sleep marketing. Marketing isn't an avocation, it a vocation. You need smart, dedicated people with well-developed skills, not just bodies.

The second thing you have to do when you are arguing with financial types is have facts and figures at hand. You have to show that marketing works and that putting money into your marketing department is a profitable investment. To do this, you have to create profit and loss statements for all of your brands and all of your activities and fully load them with all of your costs, including overhead and everything else. Then, using them, you can rationalize hiring people the same way you can rationalize and support the idea of building a new factory or warehouse.

If you have concrete data that show that sales and profits rise and fall when marketing rises and falls, and if the people running the company have any sense, you should eventually be able to carry the day. If not, my advice is that you find a new job because you are working for a company that is run by people who either aren't very smart or don't really want to succeed. Who wants to help a D player become a C player, when you could help a B player become an A or A+ player? If your company isn't willing to invest in marketing, how is it ever going to grow? By inertia?

Not likely.

Hire the Best, Then Find Them a Job

Okay, so assuming that you do get the go-ahead to hire an army of good people, let's talk about how you do that and how you have to organize the marketing department. How do you decide which people to hire? And how do you get them to work for you? Well, again, you need a strategy.

My philosophy is one that I borrowed from the famous football coach Tex Schramm. Unlike other coaches, Tex Schramm didn't go out looking for the best tackles, and ends, and running backs. Instead, he went out looking for the best athletes

"People who are really, really good at their jobs aren't exactly available. . . . So you have to find ways to make them available."

that he could find, and then he developed them into the positions he wanted them to play.

This is how we hired people at Coca-Cola. We looked for the best people. We didn't recruit for the person who had 7.6 years of experience, or had worked 2.6 years in soft drinks or had lived in 3.2 countries, or had 2.6 kids. We looked for the best marketing people in the world and then found jobs for them. We even created jobs when necessary until the right job was available. I ended up having four or five special assistants at one time because when I found someone who was very smart that I didn't have a specific job for yet, I would invent a job and put them to work on things that I wanted to develop. Pretty quickly, the exposure these people got sucked them out into the field. They were absorbed at a pace that was scary. When you find good people, hire them. If they really are good, they will find ways to add value no matter where you put them.

One problem that you will find in hiring these people is that usually people who are really, really good at their jobs aren't exactly available. By that, I mean that their employers are usually pretty happy with them and often are even paying them nice salaries. So you have to find ways to make them available. You have to find out what it is that they want but are not getting in their current jobs and then give it to them. You have to give them what I call virtual compensation. Maybe they are looking for a sense of adventure, or a place where their family will be comfortable. Perhaps someone wants their child to be born in country x or y. Or maybe it is a woman who has a boyfriend in France and wants to move there to get married. I've had people give me all of these as reasons why they might be willing to change jobs. And we accommodated all of them. We adjusted and adapted. We were extraordinarily flexible in offering people what they wanted, and in return we got what we wanted: a lot of eager, dedicated, smart people who appreciated the fact that we were willing to accommodate their needs.

Get a Blood Transfusion

As you build up your department by bringing in smart people from outside the company, you have to be really careful about

---

"We did have a lot of good people. We just needed more, and we needed ones who had skills that we didn't already have."

---

communicating with and nurturing the people already inside the company. It's similar to when you introduce a new product; you need to keep marketing the old one. I mention this because good communication is essential, and I learned that the hard way.

Shortly after I came back to Coca-Cola in August 1993, I got Doug Ivester, Coca-Cola's president, and chairman Roberto Goizueta to agree to hire fifty more people because we didn't have the people we needed to take us to our destination. I was delighted because it was going to give us a lot more marketing muscle. But all of a sudden I found that I had a revolt on my hands, and it was coming from the people I thought would be pleased like me. It came from the people I already had in the department, who were going to get a lot more resources, and from the headhunters, who stood to earn a lot of money helping me find the new ones.

The problem within the department was that I hadn't done a good job of explaining what we were doing. People thought that we were indicating that we didn't think we already had good people. And they were worried that we were going to fire them. When we finally got to the bottom of the problem, I could see how the current employees might have misunderstood. But I never did figure out the headhunters.

I would have thought that the recruiters would have loved an open-ended invitation just to find fifty good people. But they didn't. If you have one job that you are looking to fill, if you are looking for, say, a promotions manager for Singapore, you can give the headhunters a job description, which they then take and try to meet. But what happens when you say, "I don't have any specific job in mind. I just want good marketing people?" They looked at us like we were idiots. They couldn't understand what we wanted if we didn't give them a job description.

Leslie Reese, my executive assistant at the time, became director of recruiting. She used to come into my office pulling her hair out, telling me the recruiters around the world didn't want to do it. In fact, they even helped stir up the problems within the company by talking to the local management and telling them that we were hiring people behind their backs. Then the local manager would call us up in a furious panic, asking, "But what job is this for? I don't need to hire anyone; I have every job filled. Why are we doing this?"

So we had to spend a lot of time explaining. We weren't upset with the people we currently had, and we weren't about to throw a bunch of them out of their jobs. Further, just because we hired somebody in Zurich didn't mean that we were going to leave him or her there. Rather we were just expanding. We did have a lot of good people. We just needed more, and we needed ones who had skills that we didn't already have.

We already had enough people with experience in soft drinks. What we needed were people from other industries and other disciplines so that they could teach us what they knew. As Roberto Goizueta put it, "What we are looking for is people to give us a transfusion of their blood, rather than us giving them a transfusion or getting a transfusion of our own blood." It was a brilliant comment because this meant that instead of indoctrinating people, training them for six months, teaching them to throw out everything that they had learned in other businesses, we wanted people to come in and teach us what they knew, how they operated. We needed to know how we could do what we were doing in a better way based on outside knowledge.

You Can Never Have Too Many Productive People

One of the problems that the recruiters kept complaining about was that we didn't give them enough specs. My point of view is

"It is very inefficient when you have to go out and hire somebody to fill a position or do a job that you needed done five minutes ago."

that, as you look to the future, you shouldn't worry about specs. Find yourselves the best practitioners. Find out who the best media, advertising, marketing, and brand people are and hire them. There are not that many out there. A lot of companies confuse tenure with knowledge, thinking that someone who worked in a job for twelve years has valuable experience. Believe me, a lot of them do not. It is hard to find the good ones, the ones who have the ability to reinvent themselves and do the things that you need them to do, which is all of the things I have talked about for the last eight chapters. If you don't hire them when you find them, you will never develop the depth and bench strength that you need.

Look at sports teams. A baseball manager hires six pitchers even though he only needs one at a time. And he will have four more on the second team, and six more on the third team. Managers are constantly building this position up because they know that pitchers eventually get tired. In companies, we don't do this because we are concerned with head count. When we tell Wall Street that we're reducing head count, they are usually pleased because they think that we're becoming more efficient. Well, the truth is that you're usually not becoming more efficient. That's because it is very inefficient when you have to go out and hire somebody to fill a position or do a job that you needed done five minutes ago. You have to have reserves.

You need to operate on the assumption that more people properly positioned with the right objectives will produce and sell more stuff, and if this happens you will make more money and they will pay for themselves. When they don't pay for themselves, reduce the number of people you have, because they are not creating growth in the marketplace. You can't keep adding people forever, and it's perfectly okay to cut the number of people you have. But you should only cut people because they are not producing, and not because you have some arbitrary head count number. If all the people you have are producing sales and growth, when you decide to cut some of them, you are also deciding to cut your revenue. You can never have too many productive people.

Let Them Do Their Stuff

Of course, once you have hired all the good people in the world, you still have to manage them. Or, rather, you have to

> **"If you hire a bunch of people because of the knowledge that they have . . . you are going to have to listen and delegate."**

create a system and an environment where they can flourish and do all of the things that you hired them to do. This means that you have to give them responsibility and authority. You have to trust them. I really do attribute most of my success in this business to hiring good people, listening to their ideas, and letting them go at it. Whenever they made a mistake, as long as they recognized the mistake and learned from it, I let them throw that one out and come up with another one.

I hired hundreds of people at The Coca-Cola Company who were the brightest, most innovative people in the world. And when I hired them, I knew that each one of them had a little dream, a little fantasy, a promotion they wanted to do, and a positioning they wanted to establish. If you provide the environment in which they can test out their dreams, they are going to be eager, energetic, happy, and productive.

Most people like to say that they are very good at listening or at delegating, but many of them are not. If you hire a bunch of people because of the knowledge that they have, however, you are going to have to listen and delegate. Otherwise, there's no reason to pay for their knowledge.

You hire from the outside, rather than just promoting from within, because you want a transfer of knowledge. You want to learn from their successes and mistakes and spread that learning to your other people. And in order to do that, you will have to make sure that you have clear communication. You have to create a common language, and you have to delegate. Sometimes, even if you know that someone is going to make a mistake, you have to let them make the mistake so that they and their colleagues can learn from it.

Be Clear about Decision Making

Every single direct report I had at Coke had full authority to do what they needed to do. We had a system for making it clear who had responsibility for something and who was going to get to make a decision. Together with the help of a friend of mine,

**"Don't be afraid to say no.
People are not excited about your 'maybes.'"**

Bill Boggs, we invented the system, which is based on five levels of decision making. Level 1 was my decision without your input, level 2 was my decision with your input, level 3 was our decision, level 4 was your decision with my input, and level 5 was your decision.

Level 1s were the policy issues. Companies have centralized financial obligations to the shareholders, and therefore, they have to have a centralized strategy with the centralized ability to capitalize on opportunities. If you are the keeper of a trademark, or a company, or a P&L, or a balance sheet, there are certain things that you have to make decisions about that are consistent with your stewardship, and the responsibility has been bestowed upon you by the shareholders or the board of directors of the company. Those decisions have to be clearly communicated. There is nothing wrong with saying to someone, "Listen, this is a level 1 decision. We are not going to do that, whatever that is, and therefore don't even waste time trying to change it."

In fact, clearly saying no is one of the most important and difficult things that good managers do. I'm not saying that they veto things just to show how powerful they are. But it is also a manager's job to make sure that people utilize their time effectively and efficiently. One of the greatest compliments I ever got came from Tom Long, one of my direct reports at Coke. When he remarked one day that I said no a lot, I thought at first that he was complaining. But then he said, "After debating aggressively the issues and the things that I want to do, it is really reassuring to me when you finally say, 'No, we're not going to do that for the following reasons' and you explain it to me, at which point I stop wasting time and I concentrate on the yesses."

So don't be afraid to say no. People are not excited about your "maybes" or "yeah, that's an interesting thought, let me think about it," "write me a white paper," or whatever it is that you say. It's better to say yes or no. Debate it aggressively, and after you debate it at length, then just get on with the things that you need to do.

Level 2 decisions are the ones where I say, "Listen, this is going to be a level 2, I want to make the decision, but I want to make sure that I have as much of your input as possible." Write it, speak it, present it, do anything you want. At the end of the day, as long we understand exactly what you're proposing and as long as both of us know what you're thinking and what I'm thinking, then I think that I will be in a position to make the proper decision. In this case, it is critical that people understand that they have been heard, that their points of view and their analysis of a situation have been taken into account aggressively by the deciding manager. This process has the added advantage of helping people understand how you think, so that in the future they will know what it is that they are going to be judged on and how they are going to succeed or fail.

I despise Level 3 decisions. Level 3 means that all of us are going to run around and try to make a decision together. This is impossible to do. Somebody has to make the decision. Even in the strongest of democracies, somebody has to take the lead and say, "This is what we're going to do. Let's discuss it and argue about it, but somebody needs to make the decision." My goal was always to try to take every decision that was labeled as a level 3 and move it to a 2 or to a 4. Eliminate level 3 decisions whenever possible.

Level 4s are the hardest for managers because it means that you have to forget all of the power that is vested in you and let someone else take the lead. The manager gets to have input, but the other person makes the decision. It is particularly important, if you want the system to work, that you adhere to the rules and actually let the other person decide.

It's tempting to say that the other person can decide and then, if you are their manager, to strong-arm them into doing what you want. But if you do that, if you use your muscle to carry the day, or later you surreptitiously punish someone for not doing it your way, you are going to screw up the organization, because in the future, you are going to have to make all of the decisions all of the time. And many of the decisions that you make in your office in New York, or Atlanta, or London, or Des

Moines are not going to be good ones. You hire people and send them all over the world so that they can develop particular skills and expertise in particular markets. If the guy at the top makes all the decisions, you lose the benefit of the knowledge that you have developed.

Level 5 is just your decision without my input. There were certain things that people would bring up and I would say, "Listen, this is a level 5." Level 5 means that you trust people. You trust their ability, their knowledge, and their insight into what is going on in the marketplace. Level 5 means that you believe in empowerment. Essentially, level 5 says to somebody, "Listen, the reason you're here, the reason we hired you, the reason we entrusted you with the trademarks of our company, is because we believe in you. Go do it!"

Everybody's Got to Learn, and Teach

I don't mean to suggest here that I believe in hands-off management. I considered it my job to make sure that everyone fully

"It was stupid, and boring, for us to just sit there and listen while others droned on. . . . We wanted to be part of the planning."

understood the strategy, destination, and business objectives. And often I would debate quite vigorously with them to make sure that an idea fit in with the overall strategy. But my bias was always toward letting people execute. You have to let people give something their best shot. And you know what? It is my experience that people by and large are good. People have good ideas, and they want to invent, create, and discover. You just need to give them some general guidelines and the environment and leeway to let them get things done.

In the old days, the way things used to happen at Coke and still do happen at a lot companies was that the manager from the home office would fly into some market and issue a lot of orders and kill a bunch of plans. He or she was perceived to be a pain in the neck, and the goal was always to get him or her out of town as quickly as you could so that you could go back to doing what you wanted.

I'm sure that when I started making these trips that I was considered an especial pain in the neck because I didn't just issue orders. Instead, I challenged and questioned and argued. I did this in part because I wanted to make sure that people really understood the objectives and because I wanted to push them to come up with not just a good idea but with the very best idea possible. But I also did it because I believe in learning. I believed the people that we had in the different parts of the world were brilliant, were fantastic people, and I wanted to learn from them. And I knew that with my years of experience, I had a lot to bring to the table that they could learn from me. Meetings need to be exchanges of ideas. Otherwise, there's no reason to hold them. You can save time and cut costs by just sending faxes and e-mails.

Doug Ivester and I used to run budget sessions at Coke that we liked to think of as Socratic dialogues, although many of the people who attended them might have described them as scold sessions. What we decided was that it was stupid, and boring, for us to just sit there and listen while others droned on with charts and slides and presentations about plans they had already made. We wanted to be part of the planning, so we would repeatedly interrupt and ask questions and make suggestions. Many people didn't like this at first. But when they figured out that we weren't attacking them but rather trying to help them, they stopped being defensive, and we got some great new ideas out of the sessions.

You have to recognize and help everyone else recognize that aggressive interaction with people, strong debates, arguments, even violent discussions are good because they nudge people to come up with better ways to do things that they think they are already doing fine.

I have to admit that when I was younger and my bosses used to question me, I was as fast as anybody to get my back up. But over the years I have come to understand that the guys sitting at the table reviewing my plans have the ability to transfer knowledge to me that I don't have. Somewhere in the world, someone may have come up with an idea that these guys heard that could help me make my idea a little bit better. This is learning, this is knowledge, and this is incrementalism and transformation. It is using everything you can in order to make what you're doing a little bit better.

I remember how thrilled I was after about two years of holding meetings like this when people finally started saying, "Wow, that meeting was really great. You really tried to help us out." I used to laugh and tell my executive assistant, Dick Flaig, "What did they think I was doing the last time around, trying to destroy the business?"

Learn that Responsibility Goes with Authority

Implicit in this system of open communication and being clear on authority is having clarity about responsibility. When you

> **"Everyone talks about how x, y, and z are going to happen, and they get lost in the shuffle."**

determine whose decision something is, you are also making them accountable for getting the decision implemented. How many times have you been to a great meeting where everybody talks about the initiative that you are going to have, and then nothing happens? In the past, I believe that one of the biggest hindrances to success has been that great ideas don't have managers specifically delegated to get them implemented. Too often, everyone talks about how *x*, *y*, and *z* are going to happen, and they get lost in the shuffle because the people that are at the top of the decision-making chain of command move on to something else.

When you designate someone as the decision maker, you are also saying that it is his or her job to follow through. Yes, they can delegate the implementation to someone else, but it is still their job to make sure that the other person gets it done. In any organization, but especially in a big organization, you have to be very clear about who is doing what.

Think Globally, Act Locally

While I definitely believe that you have to have a centralized strategy, centralized destination, and centralized business objectives, I am just as firm a believer in decentralized execution and tactics.

> **"In each market, you need to build local organizations under local managers who can speak to local customers."**

You cannot make business decisions in New York if you want to sell products in a hundred countries, or even in all fifty states, because every market is different. Your competition is different, the economic environment is different, and the consumers are different. In each market, you need to build local organizations under local managers who can speak to local customers.

Anybody who has traveled or studied history knows that the French are different from the Italians, Mexicans are different from Guatemalans, and Brazilians are different from Argentines. Even though they may share borders and some have common languages, each country has its own superstitions, myths, history, demographic makeup, economy, and problems. All of these things make up the fabrics of these countries. And it is on these fabrics, or canvases, that you have to paint your brand and make sure that it fits and connects with the people in that market.

The only way to do this on an ongoing basis is by having local management, a local agency, a local promotion house, local manufacturing, and a local wholesaler and trucks that deliver your stuff to the stores. You also need a local manager for merchandising, local POS in the local language, and an ongoing study of exactly what is going on in those markets to make sure that you are connecting with consumers all of the time.

Sometimes, when you go into a new country, you can be blinded by initial demand. You may open a store and end up selling some, but that's usually because you are picking low-hanging fruit. This is the volume that the country is going to give to you because they know about you from somewhere else, whether you are a cigarette company, a soft-drink company, an airline, or what have you. But if you don't explain yourself in their terms, your sales are probably going to dry up, and you are definitely never going to grow.

I remember, without a great deal of joy, our entry into the Eastern European markets. We had the vision, when the Berlin Wall fell, that we could enter those markets and compete through distribution. We believed that all we needed to do was make the product available. In those days, we used to talk about availability, affordability, and acceptability, the three famous As. This basically said that you had to be accepted, which meant consumers wouldn't spit you out. You had to be affordable, which meant that consumers could buy you, and you had to be available, which means that you were within arms' reach of desire. If you had these three things, consumers would actually buy you. It worked for a while because we were getting benefits from these, but what happened very quickly is that consumers were sitting there saying, "Okay, I get it, I'm buying all of this stuff from you, why should I buy more?" When competition came in to the market and offered an alternative, they went back and forth.

I remember ten and fifteen share point swings, which scared the hell out of me, because it told me that we didn't have a consumer franchise. The reason for this was that we hadn't thought enough about the market. We didn't have the local management that we needed. We didn't have the consumer information that we needed, and we didn't really understand the economy and the politics of the marketplace. We didn't have the local experience with consumers to understand what was motivating them, and as a result, we had big problems.

In order to survive and grow, you have to get more and more people to buy your stuff more and more often, and in order to do that you have to interpret your brand for them in their culture. You have to be willing to make the investment, and to hire the people in each one of these places. When we did this at Coke, the result was that we knew what was going on in each of our markets, and we were able to aggressively change what we were doing on a market-by-market basis.

A key point here is that the only way we knew when and what to change was by setting up every market as its own business. This allowed us to see when our efforts were effective and when we were just wasting money. It also helped us figure out how many marketers we needed. Because we had profit and loss statements for every brand in every market, we could measure expenditures against earnings. If you can use people productively, what do you care how many of them you have? You just have to know when you are being effective and when you aren't. You can't do that if you don't keep score.

Over time, you may want to develop some regional or even global programs. But you should only do that if it increases business, and the only way to build programs that do that is to develop local markets first. You must go local before you can even think about going global.

Reward Excellence

I believe that compensation systems have to be commensurate with performance. We have to move more and more toward

"Unfortunately, companies often give, and employees expect, rewards for good consequences but no punishment for bad ones."

punishing mediocrity and rewarding excellence. My systems were always based on the fact that my salary was what the company paid me for showing up to do my job. A bonus was for doing something above the line of duty, and stock was for furthering the wealth of the shareholders of the company. A lot of people who had been getting stock for years got angry with me when I stopped giving it to them. But my feeling is that compensation needs to be tied to performance, otherwise it will have no value in generating the performance that you want.

American enterprise has become socialistic in its nature. Companies have gotten confused over the years, thinking that performance means tenure. Someone who is in a job for eighteen years keeps getting promoted to bigger offices, bigger salaries, bigger bonuses, and bigger stock options only because they have been there forever, regardless of performance. I think this is ridiculous.

My fundamental belief about marketing, actually about life, is that everything you do has consequences and that the person who produces those consequences should be rewarded or punished for them. Unfortunately, companies often give, and employees expect, rewards for good consequences but no punishment for bad ones.

Anytime somebody is given an assignment or project, or is hired for a job, there are certain expectations on performance. We expect them to do something for us in exchange for the money and the perks that we're willing to pay them. But if consequences are not put in place, then there is no way you are actually going to improve on what you are doing.

I always argue with my kids about service in restaurants. They give me a real hard time when we're sitting in a restaurant and we're getting terrible service, and then when it comes to tipping, I don't tip fifteen percent. They say that I'm embarrassing them because it's an accepted practice that you're supposed to tip fifteen percent.

I remember a few years back, my mother was in town and we went to an Indian restaurant in downtown Atlanta, and we had horrendous service. The food was cold, the waiter brought the wrong beverages, and he mixed up the whole service. There were about eight of us, and it was an absolute debacle. So at the end of the meal, the restaurant added an automatic eighteen percent service charge because there were eight of us and the rule on the menu read that if there were six or more, they would add the automatic eighteen percent on the bill. I called the manager over to my table and said, "Take if off," and he said, "No, it says here that we're going to add eighteen percent for parties of six or more for service." I said, "Yeah, you got it—I didn't get any service, please take it off." If I hadn't done this, then that restaurant owner would have stolen my money and kept serving cold food and having lousy service.

How many times have you been bumped from a flight? How many times has an airline canceled your reservation without letting you know? Or how many times have they overbooked, and you arrive only to find that they've bumped you? What do they do? They apologize. But more than that, when they overbook the flight today and they ask you to get off the flight, they give you a free ticket. You've been there. Somebody says, "We're overbooked by six, who wants to get off? You can get on the next plane and you can get an extra ticket." Those are consequences. The airline recognizes that they actually made a mistake, and they are actually compensating you for something they did wrong. I know that there are federal rules that require them to do that, but I am in a hundred percent agreement.

I am definitely not saying that you should get rid of somebody as soon as you think that they are not doing their job, even though this may mean that I am too soft when it comes to firing people. I think that companies have to have compassion and they have to allow for people to make mistakes and have a year where they don't perform well. But I also think that these people need to be given direct feedback and told clearly where and how they are falling short. And I am advocating that if they aren't doing their jobs well, you don't reward them.

Bonuses and stock options have become almost part of the main package of salary. I think it's a terrible mistake. People should not get bonuses and stock options just for showing up. My philosophy is that you have salary for the job that you have been contracted to do, whatever your position is in the organization. Then bonuses come for extraordinary performance, when you do something that is beyond the line of duty. Stock options should be a way to compensate you for increasing the value of the company, and a symbol that the company wants you to stay there for a long period of time, contributing aggressively to the business. This means that if in one year you do an extraordinary job, the company should compensate you better. It should give you more stock options, a larger bonus, regardless of what the formula is for bonuses. But it also means that if you don't do a good job, you should be punished by not getting the options and not getting the bonus.

One of the main benefits of this is that it helps you create a performance-driven organization as opposed to a belonging-driven organization. It just burns me up when I talk to people who say to me, "Well, I'd really like to work for this organization." It irks me because what they are saying is that being part of the organization or the corporate family is more important than doing exciting and valuable work. Belongers are people who just belong to an organization and do not feel that they actually work for the company or have a responsibility, fiduciary and intellectual, to make sure that the company succeeds in the endeavors that it is in. I don't want any belongers. I want working partners.

Everybody's in Marketing

So far, I have just been talking about hiring and rewarding people in the marketing department, but in actuality marketing is a

"Sell the system and they will sell the product."

function that belongs to everyone in the company. Every contact that consumers have with your company and your product is going to affect how they feel about you. Therefore, everybody in the company is, in a sense, in marketing.

The person who answers or doesn't answer the phone, or the person who programs and maintains the computer that answers or doesn't answer your phone. The truck drivers, who are polite or aggressive. The manufacturing people, who are or aren't careful in making the product. The financial folks, who pay or don't pay bills fairly and on time. The people in purchasing, who keep or don't keep their bargains. All of these people talk to their friends and relatives. All of them have a direct impact on potential consumers' decisions to buy or not buy your product. So you have to make sure that they are part of your marketing team. They have to be fully informed, on board, and motivated to help you out. In other words, sell the system and they will sell the product.

Although I haven't put in a section specifically labeled "Precise Communication," everything that I said about how to run a marketing department was predicated on the fact that you have to communicate and make sure that everyone unequivocally understands the destination and the strategy.

During the Gulf War, the coalition was put together on the basis that Saddam Hussein needed to be thrown out of Kuwait. The objective was very clearly stated. The interesting thing about this is that the press was charged with chronicling the reactions of the soldiers. They decided to do what they did in the Vietnam War, which is to stick a microphone in front of the soldiers to get those expected reactions, which were "I really don't want to be here, I want to go home" or "I miss my wife," etc. They were shocked to find that actually every soldier said, "Hey listen—we know exactly why we're here. We're going to kick Saddam out of Kuwait, and once we do that, we can go home." In Vietnam, nobody knew why they were there, and they were complaining about this. In the Gulf War, the commonality of purpose and clear communication served as a way of making sure that people had the proper morale, and they knew where they were going.

In business, everyone has to know what the marketing goals and the positioning and the consumer offering are so that they can pull together with you to get where you want to be. And this is true not only in the marketing department but also everywhere in the company. Everybody should have the responsibility to come up with ways to convince more consumers to buy more products or use your service more often, so you can make more money.

Communicate, Clearly and Precisely

The future of any organization is really going to be based on precise communication, on understanding unequivocally what the rules of the game are and then operating in that environment. The ability to succeed will be on the basis of getting a lot

> ## "Make sure that people understand that marketing is too important to be left solely to the marketing guys."

of stuff done, which means that you need a lot of people acting quickly, creatively, and independently. With precise communication, you will be successful. Without precise communication, you will have a hodgepodge of people running around, pulling in all directions. And even if you have very smart people, they will be doing smart things that counteract the smart things that other people are doing. It's a recipe for chaos.

When I think about selling the system on my marketing strategies and plans, I think about it the same way I think about marketing my products to consumers. I have to make the offering clear and the reasons for doing it attractive. I have to dimension it so that people all over the company understand their role in carrying us forward, and I must communicate in a variety of ways. In other words, I develop a strategy, just like I develop a strategy for everything else.

Throwing a bunch of commercials on a screen in a big auditorium in my opinion is not the way to go. You can't just throw the same messages at all of them, and you can't communicate through the same media. You must devise specific activities that will allow for the different audiences in the company to perform and to understand what it is that you are trying to do. Just as you think about addressing the different audiences of consumers, you need also to think about the different audiences within the company and among your wholesale customers, suppliers, ad agencies, and anyone else who is in a position to affect how consumers feel about your company and your product.

When I make the point that everybody is actually in marketing, I'm not suggesting that everybody should report to the marketing head or that the president of the company should always be a marketing guy—although this wouldn't be a bad idea. At the very least, as a marketer, you need to be conscious of the multiplicity of audiences that you have, and make sure that people understand that marketing is too important to be left solely to the marketing guys.

At the same time that marketers are enlisting people in other parts of the company to help sell the products that the company is producing, marketers also need to take a bigger leadership role in determining what products the company decides to produce. In the old days, the scientists or manufacturing would come up with a product and give it to the marketing guys, and tell them to go sell it. Sometimes that has worked. Post-it notes and Teflon are prime examples of inventions that the marketers then figured out how to sell. But in the future, businesses need to think about moving in the opposite direction. The marketers who know the market need to step up more often and say: "Here's what I can sell. Go make it."

Basically, I don't think that there is any company that is in the manufacturing business. Companies may manufacture or produce something, but as I see it, they are in the marketing business, because no one makes money manufacturing anything. They only make money selling that something. Airlines don't make money by having a great route system. They only make money when consumers actually buy the seats on the planes that fly those routes. Car companies don't make money by manufacturing cars. They make money by selling those cars. Cement companies might have the best raw materials or equipment, but they don't make money unless they sell the cement. It's the same everywhere, and therefore everyone in the company has to be focused on finding ways of selling more of what you make and making more of what you can sell in order to make more money for the shareholders. All of this has to be done in an overt manner; it cannot be done by accident. People have to understand their role in the overall scheme of things in order to be part of the marketing effort.

Listen to the Experts

Let me make clear here that when I say that everyone is in marketing, I still believe that you have to have clear lines of responsibility and you can't mush things together. That's a big mistake that companies make when they set up cross-functional teams. As far as I can tell, the only thing that most cross-functional

"As far as I can tell, the only thing that most cross-functional teams produce is increased consumption of club sandwiches."

teams produce is increased consumption of club sandwiches. I do believe in teamwork. You need to get the input of everyone who has something important to say and to make sure that everyone understands what he or she needs to do to sell more things. But you can't have meetings where the technical people are opining on the marketing execution for a commercial or promotion, or the legal folks are talking about positioning and branding. Meetings like this are just an absurd waste of time.

You need to figure out from the technical person what he or she can do to improve on the technical development or manufacturing of the product or service. And you want the legal people to help you fine-tune your efforts so that you don't step over any legal or ethical limits. You do want to create a team in the sense that you have people with unduplicated skills working toward the same general objective. But what you do not want is a group of people with no marketing skills commenting on marketing activities or tactics or strategies. It is the responsibility of the marketers and no one else to come up with the strategies and tactics. That's what they are paid to do.

Whenever people tell me that I am being too rigid about this I always ask: "How happy would the lawyers be if the marketers challenged their legal evaluation of an idea, project, or recommendation that you make. Their answer will immediately be, "Well, the law says. . . ." The same thing applies here. Their opinions are valid but only in their field of expertise.

In order to succeed in the future, you need to hire lots of good smart people and build a marketing department in which those people have the opportunity and the responsibility to do smart, creative things. But, as I say all the time, marketing is too important to be left to the marketing guys alone. So you also have to get everyone in the company working with you. To do this, you must have clear lines of communication and make sure everybody, both within the marketing department and outside, understands unequivocally why they are there and how they win.

When you do this, you accomplish two things. One is that you create an environment in which everybody can make his or her own best contribution to your success. And, equally important, it furthers your goal of demystifying marketing. When people understand what you are doing, they also understand that marketing is science and not art; it's about getting returns on investments and not just racking up expenses; and it's not something that you can do away with. Marketing is indispensable. And everybody in the company has to do it.

10

I LIKE AD AGENCIES— AND SOME OF THEM EVEN LIKE ME

In all my years in marketing, dealing with advertising agencies has probably given me the most notoriety and the most grief. Mention my name on Madison Avenue and you'll get an earful. On a polite day, you would probably hear, "Oh yeah, Sergio Zyman, the Aya-Cola himself!" On a not so polite day. . . well, I don't know exactly what you would hear.

I would like to be remembered in the future as someone who made a real difference by legitimizing marketing and establishing it as a serious and essential activity in the world of business. My personal jihad is to convince people that marketing is business and that being a marketing person is being a businessperson. I hate it when companies automatically cut marketing budgets in tight times. I hate it when they make manufacturing decisions and design new products and then just hand them to the marketers to sell. And I hate it when they dismiss the ideas of intelligent and thoughtful people because they are "just marketers."

Smart marketing is smart business, and one of my missions in the world is to make sure that people know that. But, alas, after thirty years and directing billions of dollars in investments that have paid enormous returns, I'm still in many people's minds simply "the guy who screwed over the ad agencies."

So in this chapter I want to set the record straight. I want to explain why I believe the advertising industry had to change, what was wrong with the traditional structure of the corporate-agency relationships, and why I was willing to take the flak that came with doing something about it. It goes to the heart of my argument in this book that advertising and marketing are not about smoke and mirrors, magic, awards, and entertainment. Advertising and marketing are, and have to be, about selling stuff, having strategies, measuring results, and investing your money to get the best returns.

Why So Many Ad Guys Hate Me: What I Did and Why

Despite my reputation, I actually like advertising and many of the creative and energetic people in the advertising business. I

"The bombs began to explode when . . . we took Coca-Cola away from McCann-Erickson. . . . And all hell broke loose when we changed the pay system."

---

spent a number of my formative years and learned a lot about marketing when I worked for McCann-Erickson in Mexico, New York, and Japan. But perhaps because I did grow up in advertising, I understand its potential and its limitations. I know what was good and what was bad about the old agency system, and I understand the forces that motivate agencies to do the things that they do. So with some pretty firm opinions on the subject when I became head of marketing at Coca-Cola, I decided to make some changes. These decisions didn't come out of just a desire to do things differently. They came out from a desperate desire to find better ways of communicating with consumers in order to sell more Coke. I knew that great ad agencies knew how to do it very well, and I was frustrated that they weren't.

I did two big things that shook up the advertising industry. The first was that I threw out the practice of hiring only one agency to do all of the work for all of our products. The second was that I decided to end the old commission system of paying agencies based on the amount of money we spent on running the ads that they produced. Instead, I started hiring different agencies to do different things, and I began paying agencies fees for the actual work that they did to create commercials. I think the red flags went up when we hired SSC&B, instead of McCann-Erickson, which had had the Coca-Cola Company's account for forty years, to introduce Diet Coke. The bombs began to explode when, after "the CAA experiment," we took Coca-Cola away from McCann-Erickson and gave it to six different agencies. And all hell broke loose when we changed the pay system.

In part because of all the heat that I took, I was especially delighted when both GM and Procter & Gamble recently announced that they were going to start paying their agencies on the basis of fees, and several agencies said that they were going to start charging clients based on the work that they did. I think that the new system allows people to perform better and actually rewards the advertising agencies better. More importantly, I think it will improve the advertising that agencies produce. I have always believed that The Coca-Cola Company should not settle for second best and that we should have the best resources in the world all over the world.

To start, as they say, at the beginning, my fundamental premise about advertising is that it is supposed to work, and that it does work. I got this idea early in my career when I was working for Procter & Gamble in Mexico. We had this new detergent with enzymes in it, and we wanted to figure out a way to get people to stop buying the old heavy-duty detergents that they were used to and to start buying ours. So we hired a local agency, and together we came up with the name Ariel and a package with an atom's symbol on it. Then they created this brilliant ad campaign.

Now, in Mexico at the time, very few people had washing

machines. Women did the laundry and they did it mostly by hand. For the wives of the laborers and the maids of the white-collar guys who wanted perfect, pristine white shirts, this was a real heavy-duty chore. A washing machine was the dream of millions of women. So the agency, Noble & Asociados, came up with a campaign that basically said "Ariel makes any bucket into a washing machine." It showed a bucket of clothes, and as the detergent started pouring in, the bucket began to agitate, turning left and right, just like the washing machine that every woman wanted. It offered a clear performance message, and it made the statement strongly. The brand took off like crazy.

This experience immediately sold me on advertising. I got the message. I understood clearly and unequivocally that advertising can sell products. And from that understanding, I developed the conviction that, if good advertising works, there is no reason to settle or pay for bad advertising. The only reason to do advertising is because it does sell products. Otherwise, it's pointless.

I have never forgotten that lesson.

A Brief History of Advertising

Unfortunately, along the way, a lot of people in the advertising business did forget it. There are a couple of reasons for this. One is that in the early days of advertising, when small merchants and entrepreneurs figured out that they could sell more stuff if they advertised, these clients didn't have marketing departments and really didn't know much about advertising. They could see that if they opened a flower shop on the corner,

"They forgot that . . . their primary purpose was to create ads that would deliver results."

they got more customers if they put a sign out in front, and that they got even more customers if they sent out flyers and ran ads that said "Hey, I've got a flower shop on the corner. The flowers are fresh. They are real pretty, and the prices are fair." If you told people that your product was available and explained to them why they should buy it, they would. But the entrepreneurs running the flower shops were too busy ordering roses, tying ribbons, and hiring delivery people to spend much time learning to advertise. They needed outside help.

So the ad agencies sprang up, and as they did, they not only became the experts on media, creative design, and production techniques, but they also developed the tools for doing consumer research and became the de facto marketing arms for their clients. The advertising agencies were really the people who developed the early theories about positioning and marketing strategies, and they told the clients what they should do.

Throughout this whole process, the advertising agencies built on the fact that their clients were pretty much in the dark about what they did. This was the period when they developed the whole self-important mystique about marketing being an unmeasurable art. "Trust me. Pay me. I will do very important things for you that you can never do yourself," they said. "But you will never understand them. And you can't measure them. So don't even try."

Meanwhile, as the advertising agencies were building this myth and pushing this hokum off on their clients, they made the big mistake of beginning to believe it themselves. To get more money, they branched out into writing speeches for the annual meetings, setting up conventions, doing public relations, and becoming "full-service" agencies. They thought that in doing this, they were making themselves more indispensable to their clients, and maybe at the time they were. But in their rush to diversify, they lost interest, or at least their focus, on advertising. They forgot that advertising was supposed to actually sell stuff and that their primary purpose was to create ads that would deliver results. Advertising became just one of a portfolio of things that the agencies did.

Awards Don't Sell Products

I watched it happen. Over the years, as the agencies grew and media technology got flashier and flashier, they continued to

"They go to Cannes and get their friends and colleagues to judge their own ads, and that is how they get public recognition."

compete with one another for clients, but instead of competing on the basis of how good they were at selling products, they began to compete on the basis of other things. "We are big and important because we have lots of billings." Or, "We have other big, important clients, so if you want to be big and important, you need to hire us." And, worst of all, "Our commercials win lots of awards from the industry panels (on which we ourselves sit), and our ads are creative and sexy and on the cutting edge. Wow! We're tops."

They were now competing and judging themselves on attributes that were totally irrelevant to what the client needed, which was to sell products. I believe that the growth of the industry awards system is the other big reason that agencies lost their way, because it made glitz, creativity, and production values the tests of good advertising, and it left effectiveness out of the equation.

Now, effective advertising does need creativity and good production values, and I don't have anything against advertising agencies holding competitions, strutting their stuff, and winning awards. I understand that when a product does well in the marketplace, it is usually the client, the manufacturer, who gets the credit. The agencies don't have a lot of ways of getting public recognition. That's why the advertising community has come up with all of their self-congratulating systems. They go to Cannes and get their friends and colleagues to judge their own ads, and that is how they get public recognition.

I think this is great. I think that agencies should get recognition from their peers for good work. My problem with this is that awards are generally based on how well an agency produces interesting images, and awards and interesting images don't sell products. I can tell you stories all day long about all of the brands that have tremendous awareness, that won the Super Bowl awards, and that lost sales for the year. When is the last time that you saw a post–Super Bowl study that measured purchase intent?

Advertising has to connect with consumers by communicating to them the benefits of the product. It's not about image and hoping that sales come later on. That's hope marketing. Advertising needs to be about developing a strong strategy that comes out of the essence of the product, and then taking that strategy and communicating it in an aggressive form. "This is why you should vote for me. This is why you should buy this product. This is why you should buy a lot of it and not just put it in your pantry, but use it." That's how you sell stuff, and that is what advertising is supposed to do.

At Coca-Cola in the 1980s, when the kids were sitting on the hill singing "I'd Like to Teach the World to Sing," and Mean Joe Greene was drinking the whole big bottle of Coke, market share was not increasing by leaps and bounds. As a matter of fact, it was flat or down in the United States, which eventually led to the New Coke strategy.

If agencies want to reward themselves, that's fine. But don't get confused. Don't think that an award that an agency wins means that your brand is going to be consumed more or your service is going to be used more. Remember who awards the awards—it's the advertising people, not the consumers. And the consumers are the only people who count.

It's the Client's Strategy, Not the Agency's

If you put things in the context that I have just described, I think that my decision to start spreading Coca-Cola's business around

"Agencies can never make smart, fully informed decisions because they are never going to be fully informed."

makes good sense. I didn't think that we were getting the most effective advertising that we could get, and I wanted to improve it. Some people thought that I was just flexing my muscles and pulling some sort of power play. But that's not true. I simply wanted to sell more stuff, and I wanted better advertising to help me do that, because I knew that good advertising works.

To be fair, I have to admit that part of the purpose and the process was to take back some of the authority that had come to reside with the agencies. But I didn't do it just because I was on a power trip. I did it because I felt that as a marketer working for The Coca-Cola Company, I had an obligation to make some of the decisions that the agencies had come to think were theirs to make. The situation wasn't entirely of the agencies' making. As I explained above, the clients had allowed the agencies over the years to become the owners of strategy. Nevertheless, I found this to be ludicrous. At the end of the day, the responsibility to grow profit and increase value added for the shareholders of a company has to rest in the management of the company. The authority can be delegated, but the responsibility can't be. And I believe that if company managers have the responsibility, they need to be the ones driving the strategy and making the decisions.

When I started working for Coke in the 1970s, the advertising agency was in charge of the strategy. I remember that the research was actually done by McCann-Erickson, and the people at McCann were very smart. They would spend a tremendous amount of money doing research and come back to say, "This is the answer, here is the positioning, here is the answer in the advertising." I just didn't buy it—I didn't buy it then, and

I don't buy it today. I don't think anybody in any company should delegate strategy.

It's not just a matter of responsibility either. The managers within a company are also in a better position than their ad agencies to make strategic decisions. That's because the agencies are never going to have as much insight into or information about a company as its managers. The fact is that the agencies can never make smart, fully informed decisions because they are never going to be fully informed. This is not necessarily their fault, but the reality is that no company is going to disclose to any outsiders, even its advertising agency, all of the inside workings of the company.

So how could an agency factor in returns on overall assets, reinvestment rates, strategies for corporate growth, or resource allocation, if the company wasn't going to disclose all those things? The answer is that it couldn't. So what you often got was a disconnect between a company's goals and the advertising that it got. The agencies may have been doing their best, but they were working in a vacuum.

Of course, the situation wasn't helped by the fact that the agencies weren't exactly pushing for full disclosure and openness themselves. All the while, they were playing up the smoke-and-mirrors, advertising-is-an-unmeasurable-art bunk. Although I wasn't out to punish them for anything, I did think that their promotion of the black box concept of advertising was, in part, a power game that, if nothing else, was diverting their energies from focusing on what I needed to get done.

What's Left for the Agency to Do?

So if the corporate managers are going to take over the strategy, what is the agency supposed to do? The agency must do what it does best—what it does better than any corporate guy could ever do—which is produce ads and messages that convey the positioning to the consumer and carry out the strategy. They have the insight into consumer behavior that comes from working with many different companies. Even if they don't directly

"It's the client that figures out what to say and the ad agency that figures out how to say it most effectively."

transfer knowledge from one client to the other, they are aware of many trends, products, categories, and situations because they are constantly exposed to different strategies and different pieces of research. And they have the creative and production skills to blend all of these pieces into a total communications package. In my book, it's the client that figures out what to say and the ad agency that figures out how to say it most effectively.

Once you decide to define the roles of the client and the agency that way, then having just one agency becomes less of a critical factor. Because it's the company's strategy and not the agency's, you can still have one strategy but hire different agencies to carry it out. In my case, hiring different agencies was part of the strategy. I wanted to strongly brand each product and sell it in the most effective manner in local markets around the world.

In the old days, producing local advertising on Coca-Cola was heresy. You were supposed to use "pattern advertising," which meant that New York would create six or eight commercials and then everyone in all the markets around the world was just supposed to translate them and run them. As you probably know by now, I don't much believe in the one-size-fits-all theory.

The reason why I have been a good marketer and been able to sell so much stuff over the years is that I believe in differentiation. You can't sell sameness. You can only sell differences. And even among products and people that may seem to be alike, you have to find, or create, differences and emphasize them. So if you are in the business of creating more and more niches, you need advertising that fits each of the niches. Anything that fits everybody doesn't fit anybody very well.

I don't think that the brand Marlboro, as much as it is believed to be an American cigarette with a cowboy and the rest of the stuff, has the same molecular makeup in Chile as it does in Ecuador. I think there are certain elements that actually vary from market to market, and that gives richness to a brand on a market-to-market basis.

Hire the Best in Each Market, for Every Brand

If you have a hundred brands in 150 countries around the world, you need to talk to consumers around the world in different ways. I felt that every single one of our marketing managers around the world at Coca-Cola had a right to have a full

"It has been my experience that only about a third of the offices of worldwide agencies are first-rate."

staff for each brand and the very best advertising that he or she could find.

No single agency was the best in every market we served, or in every market it served, so no single agency could meet our needs. We needed to draw on the resources of the different agencies around the world to activate and maximize the potential growth that we had on a country-by-country basis.

Perhaps in a perfect world, one agency could be the best in every market, but it has been my experience that only about a third of the offices of worldwide agencies are first-rate. About a third are pretty good, and about a third are only okay at best. Fortunately the new breed of ad agency leaders, like John Doonor at McCann and the folks at Ogilvy are starting to fix their structures and will eventually have stronger agencies.

We also needed different agencies for each brand, because the brand manager had a right to an advertising agency that was fully committed and devoted to that brand and not to competing products, even if they were our own products. If a manager is going to maximize the sales and profits of a brand, he or she needs people who will be dreaming and thinking about that brand twenty-four hours a day, not just seven or eight.

When we started planning to work on Diet Coke, the idea was that we were going to work with McCann, the same agency that was working on Coke. At the time, we were practicing portfolio management, which means that you build a fence around each of your brands. You decide that there are certain things a subbrand or a line extension have because you don't want to highlight the weaknesses of another brand in your portfolio. The problem with this, of course, is that your competitors are smart, and while you are protecting your brands from your own other brands, they are coming in and stealing your volume. In any event, we hired McCann so it could "protect" the brand Coke by not allowing Diet Coke to say anything about Coke that was inconsistent.

But then, what happened was that right after McCann got the assignment to work on Diet Coke, the agency went back to Coca-Cola's then chairman, Paul Austin, and convinced him that it was a bad idea to launch Diet Coke. Mr. Austin sent a letter to Don Keough, who was Coke's president of the Americas and the project leader on Diet Coke, and the project was canceled.

When Roberto Goizueta was named chairman and president of the company, Don got Roberto to approve restarting the project. I convinced Don that we should go to what was then called SSC&B, and is now Lintas Ammiratti Puris. He said that it was okay, and I ran to the airport, hopped on a plane, went to New York, signed a contract with them. Before anyone knew it, I had a second agency, and it was too late to change it.

SSC&B did a great job, in part because they positioned Diet Coke without thinking once about what it would do to the Motherlode Coke. That was McCann's responsibility.

After this experience, when we decided to introduce New Coke we asked McCann to give us a number of competing teams on the brand. This generated great work, and as everyone knows, the message of New Coke was communicated in a hurry to consumers. Unfortunately, it was a message that they didn't like.

Despite their good work on New Coke, when the dust settled, we decided that McCann was not the right agency to work on Classic Coke. This was because they wanted to take Classic to where it was before New Coke. But Coca-Cola Classic had transformed itself and established a new relationship with consumers in America as a result of the New Coke uproar. We felt that it was necessary for us to have a fresh look. McCann wasn't interested. So we moved Coca-Cola Classic to SSC&B, and gave Tab and some other stuff to McCann to compensate them. This was a very painful process, but we felt that it was necessary. Unfortunately, it didn't really stick. I left the company in 1987, and it didn't take ninety days for McCann to get Coca-Cola Classic back.

The problems that we had with McCann-Erickson are illustrations of two of the things that I have been talking about. The first, in the case of Diet Coke, was that the agency was so devoted to and so protective of original Coke, that it wasn't able, or willing, to give Diet Coke a chance. The Classic Coke disagreement highlights my point that you shouldn't let an agency substitute its strategy and positioning ideas for your own. Yes, the introduction of New Coke had created an enormous mess, but the fact was that it succeeded in transforming the relationship of Classic with the public. We didn't want to take it back to where it had been before. McCann is a great agency, and for some clients it is the one that they should keep forever. But the management on our account at the time and their approach were not right for us.

The CAA Experience

When Doug Ivester became president of Coca-Cola USA just before I rejoined the company, he again decided to go outside of McCann. The company was spending money left and right, and it wasn't getting the work that it needed. So this time, the

"With CAA and all of its movie industry experience and contacts, we got a laboratory that was constantly testing new techniques."

company hired Creative Artists, which was a talent agency and not a traditional advertising agency, to do commercials. And it hired a bunch of other agencies to do other things. My personal view is that management didn't really believe that the CAA arrangement was going to work, because Doug asked me to work on a parallel project with McCann to develop an alternative campaign. Soon after the work from CAA arrived, it was apparent to me that we had a winner.

By then I was in serious and final conversations about rejoining the company, so Doug asked me to attend the session where CAA was going to present the follow-up campaign. Michael Ovitz and Bill Haber, who were CAA's two top executives, and the creative team arrived at the same time I did at the reception desk. I could tell from the looks on their faces that they were not happy to see me. But it took fifteen minutes for all of us to hit it off. These guys were great. They got it, and the course of advertising for Coke and all other brands of the company changed forever . . . or at least for as long as I was there.

The hiring of CAA brings me to the other reason why I think you need to hire a variety of agencies. No matter what anybody would like to think, every agency is better at some things than at others. Each agency has a core competence. Sure, they can work in other areas, but they are going to be especially strong in some areas. My view is that you need to match brands and the activities they need with the talents and skills of the agencies. You need to find the match between your advertising agency and the needs that your brand, product, or service has. If you don't, you end up with a mismatch.

When Coca-Cola hired Creative Artists, we did it because

they weren't a traditional agency, and their point of view on advertising was totally different. The folks at CAA, initially led by Michael Ovitz and later by a team of others, understood film. They understood all kinds of production techniques. They understood Hollywood. They understood special effects, and they understood what was current. Why was this important? It was important because consumers react to the production of films, to animation, special effects, and all the current themes in movies, whether it's melancholy, fast action, or cute little animals. With CAA and all of its movie industry experience and contacts, we got a laboratory that was constantly testing new techniques and devices to get consumers to go to the movies. CAA was able to take the consumer insights that it developed in the film business and its knowledge of production and blend them with our brand icons to produce great ads.

This was undoubtedly an untraditional way of going about it. I'm not even sure that the folks at CAA were aware of this or realized what they were doing, but they were getting insights on consumer behavior and then translating those behaviors into iconography for our brands, so that consumers bought more of our brands more often. They looked at a way to modernize the essence of the brand by utilizing skills, new techniques, and modern approaches that would address consumers. The campaign started moving the numbers dramatically.

At the same time, we hired W.B. Doner out of Detroit because they had worked for many retailers and understood retail better than anybody else. They created programs that connected Coke to consumer sentiment at specific retail seasons. For example, at Christmas, they designed twelve-packs to look like gifts to put under the Christmas tree. And they did the Christmas Caravan commercial that metaphorically showed the warmth of the Christmas season arriving as a Coke truck pulled into town and all the decorations lit up. At the busiest shopping season of the year, this made customers think of Coke. If you wanted to do something that had a retail overtone to your brand, Doner was better than anyone else.

We hired DMB&B out of St. Louis to talk to the blue-collar

market because of their tremendous expertise with Budweiser. Wieden & Kennedy, under the leadership of Dan Wieden, helped us understand how to maximize our sports affiliations. They helped us initially with cricket in India, Pakistan, Bangladesh, and other countries during the world cricket championships. Later, they helped us in soccer, American football, and baseball. They understood the consumer from that vantage point. And we hired McCann in middle Asia and Latin America for some of our brands because they were the best there.

If you look at the architecture of worldwide agencies, it is almost always the same. There were a couple of guys who left another shop or another place because they had an idea. The agencies attracted people who were strong in particular areas or wanted to work in a specific environment. They were run by the David Ogilvys and the Bill Bernbachs, who had a vision and a dream. This is how Backer Spielvogel was built—Bill Backer and Carl Spielvogel used to work for McCann-Erickson on the Miller account. Then they broke away from McCann and built their own agency. They operated out of a hotel room and had a core competence that was developed out of working on the beer business, and they extended that experience into building a big agency and a hell of a business.

Cliff Freeman understood humor really well. I think the people that he attracted to his agency were people who liked to work with humor. This came out of his years and years of working on Little Caesar's Pizza. You can't challenge BBD&O's great ideas on Pepsi, General Electric, Frito-Lay, and the others. Again, they attract creative and productive people who want to work with these sorts of companies and products.

I am not implying that agencies cannot develop different abilities, but they do have different personalities and styles. So it's very important to find a match between an agency and a brand. Cliff Freeman handles some of the products of The Coca-Cola Company and does a spectacular job. But when I consulted for Miller Brewing Company, I worked with Cliff, and I just didn't think it was a natural match, although Cliff might disagree with me.

So does this mean that you should never have a worldwide agency? Not in the least. Many times it is important to use a worldwide agency as a way to provide continuity and cascade information. If you don't have the organization in house, an advertising agency network is a way of cascading information and providing for continuity. McCann-Erickson has a fabulous network of agencies for providing just that kind of continuity. But you have to be overt when you decide to use one agency worldwide. You have to decide that you want the continuity and make sure that you are doing this for that reason. And you shouldn't do it for very long because marketing is one of your core business activities and you need marketers inside the company who can offer guidance and participate in every part of the business. An outside agency can't do that. I took Coke away from McCann and hired a bunch of different agencies because I had built a large and capable marketing department inside of Coke. I didn't need a partner to design strategy. I needed the best advertising in the world and colleagues who were able, excited, and eager to produce it.

Pay for What You Need, and Expect the Best

When I announced that I wanted to stop paying advertising agencies commissions and start paying fees, Madison Avenue had a fit. The agencies felt threatened that I would be depriving

---

**"We didn't need the social visits.
We wanted working visits that we would pay for."**

---

them on the upside. If for some reason I decided to spend a ton of money running ads, if we had an opportunity, a problem, a crisis, or whatever, they wouldn't get a piece of the action because there wouldn't be any commissions. But I argued, and still believe, that I was working in their bests interests as well as my own. I wanted to have the best creative people in the world working on my accounts. So I wanted the agencies to have a predictable cash flow so that they could hire those people. If I was removing the upside, I was removing the downside as well.

Advertising is, unfortunately, still perceived by many corporate executives to be an expense, and as long as it is seen as just an expense, companies will cut it without ever looking to see if it is working. At Coca-Cola, I was fighting that mind-set as hard as I could, but I couldn't promise that I wouldn't get in a situation where I would have to cut back on advertising because of some political or economic crisis or for some other reason. So what I wanted to do with the ad agencies was to make sure that they had a steady stream of income that would allow them to hire the right people and not have to worry about what I did in my marketing. Those who were smart understood this right away; those who were not fought it for a long time.

My feeling is that agencies need to be compensated the same way you and I need to be compensated. If you work and are productive, you should get a salary, a nice office, a bonus, and possibly stock options. I'm not necessarily for giving ad agencies stock options, but you get the point. They need to be paid for what they do, regardless of what I do. If they aren't, if they are subject to the ups and downs of my business, they will start losing money and cutting back whenever I tighten my belt. And when I am tightening my belt is just the time when I need the very best advertising. I need to get more mileage for my dollars, and I need to jump-start sales to get me out of the hole that made me tighten my belt in the first place.

When I went back to Coca-Cola, we had agencies around the world that, through a variety of schemes, were getting twenty-five percent and thirty percent commission on our billings. They would rationalize this in a specific country by saying that they were losing money in other countries. So, I said, let's make a deal where you will make money on all of the work you do for us. When we analyzed the compensation, it turned out that if we actually paid them good fees that would let them make money, our out-of-pocket would be the same, and maybe even a little bit more. But in return, we would have better advertising and they would have guaranteed profits on the work that they did for Coca-Cola.

What I told the agencies was this: Coca-Cola would pay the agency for all of the people that they put on our account (in agreement with us). We would pay a multiplying factor for overhead, and we would give them a percentage of profit beyond that, which was significantly larger than any profit they were making on any other account. Further, we said, when they did outstanding work, we would give them a bonus. Our analysis was that we would pay the salaries of the people on the account, two and a half times that amount for overhead and management, and then on top of that, we would give them twenty percent profit. I agree with David Ogilvy, who once said that if you pay your agencies in peanuts you will get monkeys.

Still, we got resistance. The very first level of resistance from the agencies was that in this system, they couldn't charge ten percent of the chairman of the board, fifteen percent of the president, ten percent of the director of strategic planning, and five percent of the secretary to each one of these people, etc., to the client. Correct. Absolutely correct. They used to send those people out to butter us up and chat with us to "maintain the relationship." Our premise was that we didn't need the social visits. We wanted working visits that we would pay for. But if the agency wanted to send the management on a social visit, they could do it at their own expense.

The next thing that happened was the agencies all loaded the list of people that were going to work on the account. Again, we said, "No thanks." We wouldn't pay for any people who did not contribute to the development of the advertising, consumer insights, or the things that we needed. We were very rigid about who would be working on the account because that's what we were actually going to mark up and give them a chance to make a significant profit on.

I didn't demand that everyone listed on the account actually do research, write copy, and produce ads. In middle Asia, for example, a list came in that included drivers and kitchen staff for the agency. Our people immediately said, "This is ridiculous!" but I said it wasn't. To do business in that part of the world, you need drivers and kitchen staff, and if the agency said we needed those people in order for them to do our work, then we should pay them on the basis of the rules that we had developed.

Eventually it worked out. The agencies understood that they had very little risk on their profitability, and pretty soon, on the basis of very good work, we ended up paying incremental bonuses to them. The way this worked was that David Wheldon, who worked for me for a while and left the company to go back to Europe, developed an agency evaluation system. The AES rewarded the agencies on the basis of their contribution to the growth of the business, and if they met certain criteria, they could get discretionary bonuses.

Nobody believed us. So David and I had great fun the very first year when we traveled to the agencies at bonus time. We would get to these meetings and the agency people would spend all kinds of time complaining about how they weren't making as much as they should. Then we would pull a check out at the end and give them a couple of million dollars. After that, it didn't take too long for people to start improving their performance.

Focusing on Results Lets Creativity Blossom

The first allies we won at the agencies were the creative people. You might think that they would have been just the ones who hated us most because we were saying that we didn't care

"Since we didn't care about anything but selling more Coca-Cola products, we were willing to try stuff that might have scared off other clients."

about smartsy-artsy advertising. We were very hard-nosed about just wanting commercials that worked. But, in a way, that made use very broad-minded and open to off-the-wall ideas. Since we didn't care about anything but selling more Coca-Cola products, we were willing to try stuff that might have scared off other clients. If something was consistent with the strategy, even if it seemed to have only the vaguest possibility that it might work, we said, "Go ahead. Try it." Even if we, ourselves, didn't particularly like it, we would say, "Go ahead. Try it." We gave them a lot more freedom than most other clients. And it paid off. Remember the Cherry Coke ads with the kid riding an ostrich in a department store?

And it didn't just pay off when we got the occasional home run, blockbuster of a commercial. It also paid off because in giving the creative people their space and rewarding them handsomely when their ideas produced results, we attracted a lot of top creative talent to our agencies and our accounts. The first time I worked for Coke, our agencies were having a tough time attracting good, creative people to work on Coke. It was very frustrating. They came out with the ad that they thought we wanted to buy as opposed to the ads that were the rights ads for us to buy.

In today's environment, every creative person that I know in every agency all around the world wants to work on Coke. Why? I think it's because Coca-Cola gives them the chance to do their thing. Coke is very clear that the strategy belongs to Coke, but the experts on creativity are the agencies. They are the people who can actually come up with the modern and contemporary connections that will allow a brand to establish a relationship with a consumer. They know how to do it, and I don't. From my vantage point, management should focus on marketing and get out of the advertising business. Don't do creative in house. Make sure you hire the best agency, pay them well, and the results will be phenomenal.

Agencies are a tremendous resource. I sometimes used Leo Burnett, for example, to help me critique campaigns created by other agencies. No, I didn't ask them to look over any shoulders and second-guess the primary agency. Rather, I asked them to help me analyze things that were working.

Unequivocally, one of the greatest advertising and strategic positioning successes of The Coca-Cola Company while I was there was Sprite. I have talked about this already, but Sprite's architecture and repositioning as a soft drink with attitude was working so well that it scared me that we were just talking to ourselves. At one point I asked Leo Burnett to evaluate for us the performance of Sprite. They did a superb job, and we paid them handsomely for it. They went at it as if they were the agency of record, but there was never any misconception or miscommunication between them and Lowe & Partners, which was actually the agency of record, with regard to what they were doing. They gave us an appraisal of why the advertising was working so well.

It helped us tremendously because we had a outside observer with no vested interest looking at a job and telling us what was good and what could be improved about it. They drew lessons that we all learned from. Competitive analyses such as these only work, however, if you have a good agency system, and if you have agencies that understand what you are trying to do. As a result, we discovered things that helped both Coke and the agencies be more successful.

I believe that the agency business as it once was is bankrupt. Agencies need to transform themselves. They need to stop focusing on the perks, the awards, the tangential "full service" work and all the trappings of big-league advertising, and they need to get back to basics. The job of advertising agencies is to produce good advertising, advertising that helps the client implement its strategy and that sells stuff, stuff, and more stuff. Some agencies have always done this. The Fallon McElligotts, the Wieden & Kennedys, and Cliff Freemans of the world are first-rate advertising agencies. And even the Ogilvys and McCanns are starting to transform themselves. They are beginning to understand that their role, which is a valued and important role, is to communicate a client's message to the consumers. If they want to peddle a lot of other services, that's fine, but only if they don't forget that they are what their name says: ADVERTIS-ING agencies.

Clients must transform themselves as well. They must take control of strategy, which means that they must actually learn to develop strategies. They need to match their brands with the agencies that will do the very best work for them in each market. They need to hire those agencies and then brief them clearly so that they understand the strategy and the goals. Then they need to pay them reliably and well so that they can afford to attract the very best talent.

If you do this, at the end of the day, you end up getting better messages, which will convince consumers to buy your stuff more often. You and your shareholders will be richer, and so will your advertising agencies.

CONCLUSION

TRADITIONAL MARKETING IS NOT DYING— IT'S DEAD!

Perhaps you are thinking that the approach to marketing that I have described in this book is not the way you want to go. And maybe you are also thinking that you'll just stick with your old ways because they are working for you. If so, I strongly suggest that you think again.

Old-style marketing is dead. It is as dead as Elvis. Perhaps its handlers have propped it up in a chair. Maybe those who depend on old-style marketing the most—the big advertising agencies and the major television networks—have wired up the cadaver to massive marketing budgets, so they get a flinch or kick out of it every once in a while. But there is no more singing and dancing. The music has died. Marketing as we have known it is over.

If your retirement party is already on the calendar, there may still be time to cash in your stock options and profit sharing and get out while old-style marketing still has some semblance of life. But it's moldering fast. So if you're planning a career horizon that goes out more than a couple of years, you'd better come up with something new, and do it fast.

Look around you. The tried and true tactics of the old marketing simply aren't working the way they used to. Like a battery that is dying, they may still generate some juice, but the power is getting weaker and weaker. The same dollar spent on the old tactics doesn't give the return it did five or ten years ago.

There's lots of evidence.

Mass advertising has lost its ability to move the masses. Technology has given people many more options than they had in the past and created a consumer democracy. Everybody has a thousand choices for any product they might want to buy, and there are a million different products competing for their wallets. So marketers increasingly need to find ways to speak to customers individually, or in smaller and smaller groups. With so many choices, each customer has many factors that weigh in his or her decisions, so marketers have to find the reasons that speak to particular customers' concerns. Old-style, one-size-fits-all mass marketing can't do this.

In reality, one size has never fit all, but when customers didn't have so many choices, they had to put up with it. Now they don't. No longer can marketers rely on retailing strategies designed to make money by forcing consumers to buy what the marketers want them to buy, when and where the marketers want them to buy it. These strategies are aimed more at wooing retailers with slotting and promotion allowances than at wooing customers, and they just won't fly anymore. In the future, retailing strategies are going to have to be like those of Amazon.com or the one-hour eyeglass shops, which are designed to sell the consumers what they want to buy. And they do it by making it easier, better, less cumbersome to do so.

Because old marketing isn't working, every year, earlier and earlier in the marketing year, people are admitting defeat and falling back on "Plan B," which is, of course, price promotion. Price promotion is definitely on the rise, and the cost of it is going up. That's because when everyone is cutting prices, you have to cut yours even more. The sale that it cost you a dime to get three years ago, now costs a quarter, and still, all you are getting is rented volume that is going away as soon as you stop paying for it.

Price promotions are like negative politics. Politicians go

negative when everything else has failed. When they are a couple of weeks away from the election and they have no platform and no relevance, they start throwing dirt at the opponent. Negative campaigns move votes because, like price promotions, they establish a difference and give the consumer a basis for making a decision. But neither price promotions nor negative campaigning do anything to build long-term support.

When a price promotion ends, the consumers move on to the next guy who's willing to pay them to buy his product. And when a politician gets elected through negative campaigning, he or she has established only that the opponent was a dog and not that there is a positive reason why the voter would want to reelect the winner. It's a very expensive, and ultimately worthless, game. Every day you can turn to the newspaper's business pages and learn that another company has succeeded to death. It has sold a lot of stuff and gone broke in the process.

In the future, marketing has to be about creating value in the minds of the consumers. This means building brands by identifying the common ground between a consumer and a product or service. It is about deepening these relationships over time. It's about defining expectations and overdelivering on them. And it is about a whole lot of other things that you have to do to keep your product fresh and desirable to consumers.

As more and more marketers realize this and get on with new marketing, the snowball is going to turn into an avalanche, because when executives see what real marketing, the new marketing, can do, they are not going to settle for anything less. So staying with old-style marketing is not an option. You cannot stand still. If you don't start moving ahead and doing things differently, you are definitely going to be left behind.

Now, becoming a new-style marketer is hard work, especially at the beginning, when you will encounter lots of resistance. Senior management will not want to give you the resources that you need, and will continue to try to cut marketing budgets when markets get weak. You have to stand your ground and come up with the facts and figures based on data and P&Ls to show that your marketing does work and that it is a good investment that pays returns. The people in your marketing department will get edgy when you push them to make their good ideas even better and when you kill their pet projects because they aren't working. And, depending on who your advertising agencies are, you are likely to find them less than eager to comply with your demand that they focus on producing brilliant ads while you control the strategy.

But trust me, there are rewards to new marketing, and they are fabulous. So persevere. The principles I've laid out in this book aren't just theories. They have been developed and used in component form in some of the most exciting and successful marketing ventures of the past fifteen years. I know that they have worked for me, and they will work for you too. Nothing kills resistance like success.

Even after the resistance dies, your job isn't going to get easy. As a new marketer, you will never get to the point where you can just sit back and prop your feet up. To succeed in marketing, you always have to work hard at it. But that's part of the fun. Who wants to sit back and watch the world go by? So jump in! The sooner you start, the more money you can make for your company and yourself.

Throughout this book, I've said that strategy and logic are key. So, here's a checklist of the strategic principles you need to remember. Using just some of them will definitely make you a better marketer, but if you use all of them, there's no stopping you.

The Principles of New Marketing

- The sole purpose of marketing is to sell more to more people, more often, and at higher prices. There is no other reason to do it.

- Marketing is serious business—and, increasingly, serious business is about marketing.

- Marketing is not magic, and marketers do themselves no

favor when they pretend that it is. There's nothing mysterious about it.

- Marketing is a professional discipline. You can't leave it to your Uncle Willie or anyone else who isn't a trained professional.

- The marketplace today is a consumer democracy. Consumers have options, so marketers have to tell them how to choose.

- Plan your destination. Make it where you want to be, not where you think you can get.

- Once you have your destination, develop a strategy for getting there.

- Strategy is the boss. Never forget it. Strategy is what controls the "everything" in "everything communicates." You can decided to change your strategy, but you can't deviate from it.

- Marketing is a science. It is about experimentation, measurement, analysis, refinement, and replication. You must be willing to change your mind.

- Figure out what is desirable and make that what you deliver; or figure out what you can deliver and make it desirable. But remember, the former is a lot easier than the latter

- Measure each brand and each marketing region. Do it regularly and often, at least monthly. Marketing must create results.

- Ask questions. Be aware, insatiably curious, and creative. Creativity really is a process of destroying old ideas, but that's okay. Every day is a new day.

- Sameness doesn't sell. The value of your product will be determined by its differentiation from the competition in ways that are relevant to the consumers.

- Build your brands by using all the elements of image: trademark image, product image, user image, usage image, and associative image.

- Use the right yardsticks: focus on profit, not volume; on actual consumption, not share of market; and on share of future purchases, not brand awareness.

- Keep giving your customers more reasons to buy. You need them to come back more often and to buy more at higher prices.

- Market locally. You have to give all your customers something that appeals to them personally. Global brands are built out of many strong local brands.

- Fish where the fish are. Concentrate your sales efforts on consumers who are willing and able to buy your product. Segment the market to help you identify your most profitable targets.

- It is significantly easier to increment behavior or broaden behavior than to teach or change behavior.

- Think S.O.B.—Source Of Business; where will your next sale and dollar of profit come from?

- Don't be blinded by visible demand. Preference is perishable. Keep selling the sold.

- Make sure everybody in your organization understands the strategy, the destination, and the business objectives. Then let them execute.

- Find the best available marketing professionals and create jobs around them. You've got to have the best people, not the best organization chart.

- Reward excellence and punish mediocrity.

- Strategy is your job. The job of your ad agencies is to communicate it effectively.

- No single agency can satisfy all of the needs of all of your brands. One size definitely doesn't fit all.

- Pay well so your agencies have the resources to attract good talent—but demand results that are clearly measurable.

- Have a sense of urgency, and work with passion. Otherwise, what's the use of getting up in the morning?

A lot of these things that I am suggesting here may seem like just obvious common sense. But when you start to implement them in the marketing world, where the traditional standards have been mystery and magic, you are going to be considered a revolutionary. So be prepared, and keep your sense of humor when people start poking at you.

I wasn't exactly thrilled about it, when some of the wags on Madison Avenue started calling me the Aya-Cola. But what the heck? I just figured that those are the fleas that come with the dog. And besides, I was going to get the last laugh, because while they were clinging to the past, I was going to build a new future. And I was going to get there way ahead of them.

INDEX

consumers (*cont.*)
  communism of, 104–6
  compared to voters, 126–27
  conversion rates of, 132–34
  democracy and, 101–3, 230,
    233
  expectations of, 79–80, 231
  happiness and confidence
    of, 62
  importance of, 96–98
  limits and, 85–87
  listening to, 60–61
  motivating to buy more,
    4–5, 12, 31, 49, 200, 234
  negative advertising and, 90
  new, 18, 25, 49, 69
  preferences of, 18
  reaction to Hollywood tech-
    niques, 219
  research questions and,
    57–58
  segmented market and,
    123–25
  social trends and behavior
    of, 95–101
  softening up, 71
  solvency of, 136–37, 152, 234
  young, 18
consumption, 121–22, 161, 234
Converse shoes, 18, 19
conversion rates, 132–34
Cosby, Bill, 56
cost-plus basis, 26
costs, 7, 56, 141, 181
  fixed, 20, 23
  of research, 54
  volume and, 25

Creative Artists Agency (CAA),
  217–19
creativity, 168–71, 172, 173,
  210, 224–27
Crest toothpaste, 145–46
cross-functional teams, 202–3
Crystal Pepsi, xv, 35–37, 151
customers. *See* consumers

D.A.D. formula, 84
data, 44–45, 54, 59, 61, 181,
  231
decision making, 187–90
defense industry, 25–26
Delta Airlines, 78
demand, 17–19, 20, 21, 234
democracy, 101–3
demographics, 53, 123, 128
destination, fixed, 48–49
destination planning, 23,
  26–27, 33, 171–72, 177,
  233
detergents, 207–8
dialogue, control of, 55–57,
  79, 87–89, 90, 110, 120
Diana, Princess, 100–101
Diet Coke, xi, 29, 35, 37, 68,
  92, 143
  ad agencies and, 216, 217
  competing against other
    Coke brands, 75
  image of, 81
  market expansion and, 152
  marketing strategy for, 149,
    150
  megabranding and, 70, 71
Diet Pepsi, 149